This book belongs to

_____

- -

_____

Grade: _____

School: _____

Sight words or High Frequency Words are the words that occurs frequently in reading and writing. This **"Dolch Pre-K & Kindergarten Sight Words Practice Book"** is the beginner's level practice book, which has all the 92 high frequency words for the kids to learn and write.

This easy-to-follow multisensory practice book is thoughtfully sequenced to build children's learning and writing ability with fun **coloring activity.**

This book helps the children to practice the sight words with spelling. This learn-to-read and write book will keep kids engage from start to finish with tracing, writing and coloring activities. This book has the basic fundamentals which improves the kids handwriting with the **dot-to-dot tracing** and motivate them to write by their own.

This book starts with practicing basic strokes, learn the sight words by tracing and writing, sight words **flash cards** for practicing & tracking the learning progress, sight words **summary chart**, and a completion certificate as a token of appreciation.

This book is suitable for Pre-K and Kindergartners.

Table of Contents:

1. Basic Strokes practice (i.e. lines and curves)

2. Dolch Pre-K Sight words

3. Dolch Kindergarten Sight words

4. Sight words Flash Cards (Pre-K & K)

5. Dolch Pre-K & K Sight words Summary chart

6. Certificate of completion

Dolch Pre-K & K SIGHT WORDS

PRACTICE BOOK
For Pre-K & Kindergarten

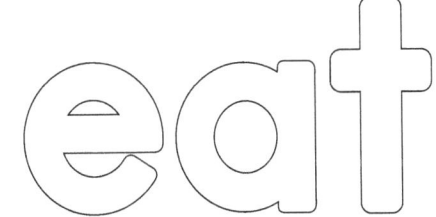

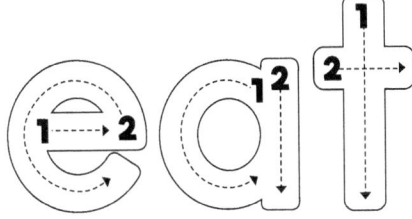

Tracing

Ages 4+

Coloring

Dear Parents,

Thank you for your purchase!

I sincerely hope, this book will be more helpful and interesting for the kids to learn **Dolch Pre-K & Kindergarten Sight Words.**

Your opinion matters to us. We'd love to hear from you! You can leave your valuable comments and **honest feedback.** Please take a moment to write a review. We appreciate your support.

Email us at abczbook@gmail.com with the title "**Dolch Sight Words Workbook**" and get your free practice worksheets!

Hopefully, your kids will enjoy this book.

Enjoy Learning!

abcZbook Press

abcZbook Press
www.abczbook.com

Basic strokes practice

Basic strokes practice

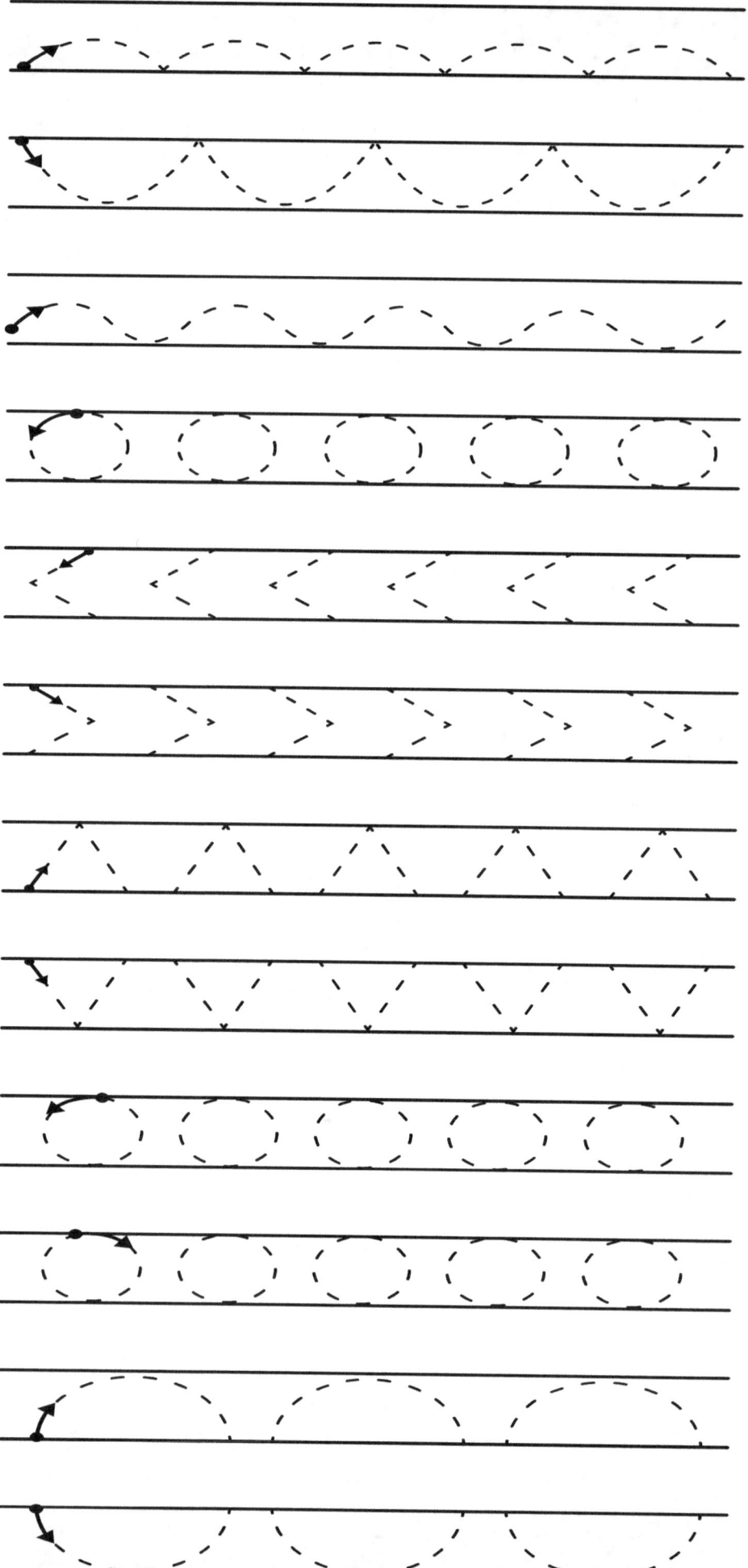

Basic strokes practice

Pre-Kindergarten

Dolch Sight Words

Read the word:

Color the word:

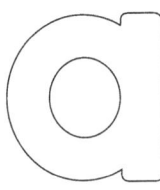

Trace the word:

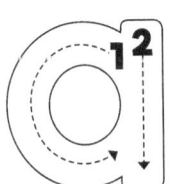

Trace the word:

Write the word:

Read the word:

Color the word:

Trace the word:

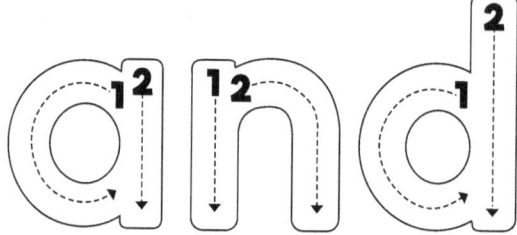

Trace the word:

Write the word:

Read the word:

away

Color the word:

Trace the word:

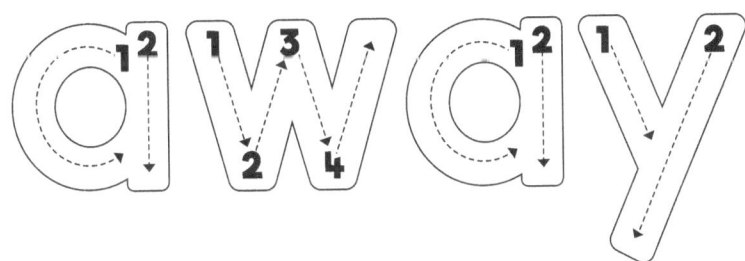

Trace the word:

Write the word:

Read the word:

Color the word:

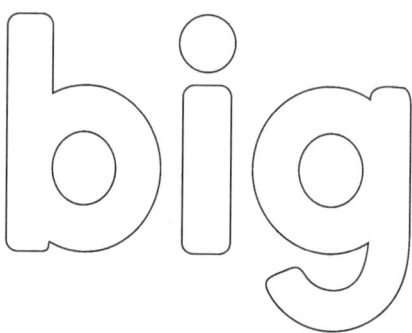

Trace the word:

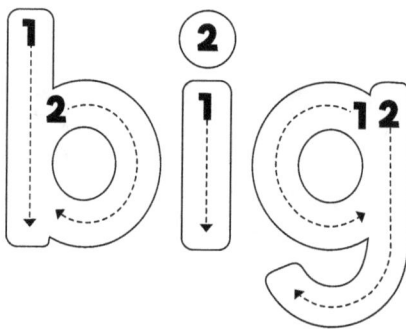

Trace the word:

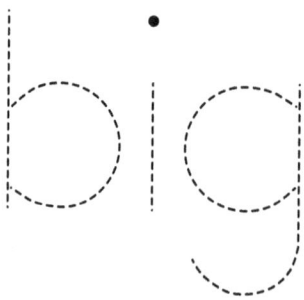

Write the word:

Read the word:

Color the word:

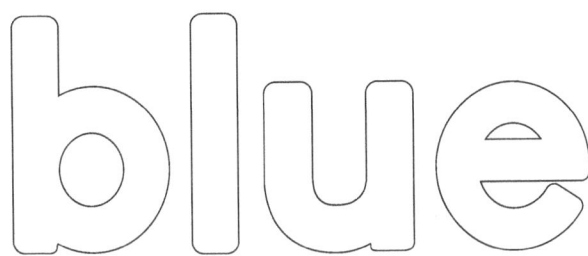

Trace the word:

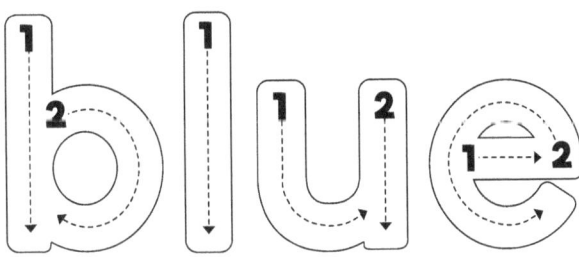

Trace the word:

Write the word: _____

Read the word:

Color the word:

Trace the word:

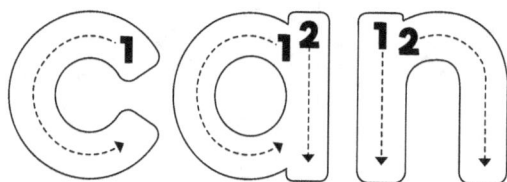

Trace the word:

Write the word:

Read the word:

Color the word:

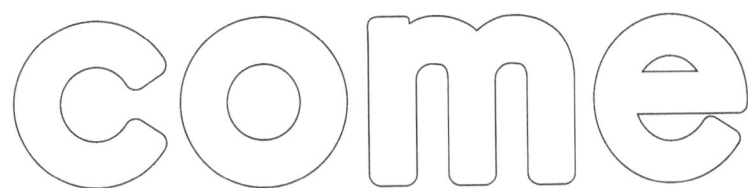

Trace the word:

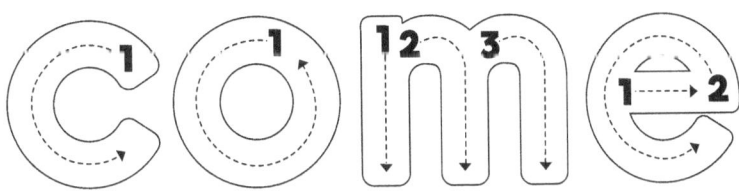

Trace the word:

Write the word:

Read the word:

down

Color the word:

Trace the word:

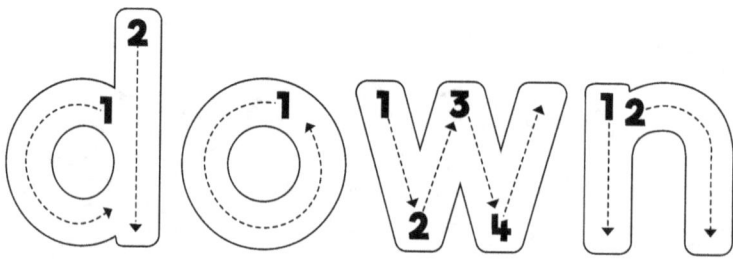

Trace the word:

Write the word:

Read the word:

Color the word:

Trace the word:

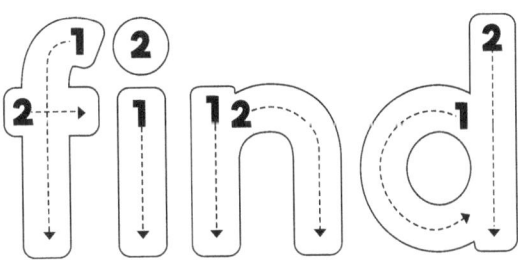

Trace the word:

Write the word: _____

....

_____

_____

....

_____

Read the word:

for

Color the word:

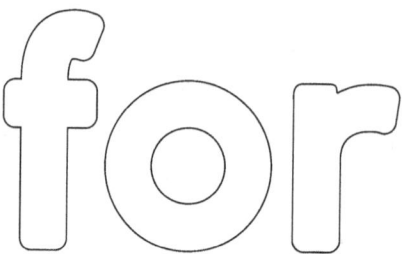

Trace the word:

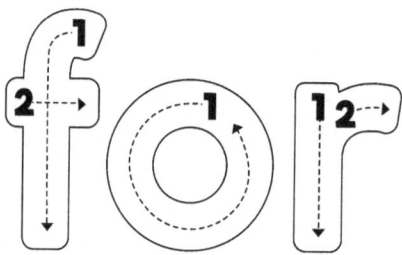

Trace the word:

Write the word:

Read the word:

funny

Color the word:

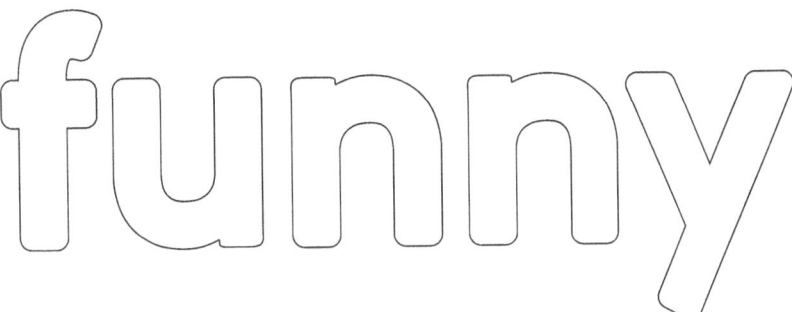

Trace the word:

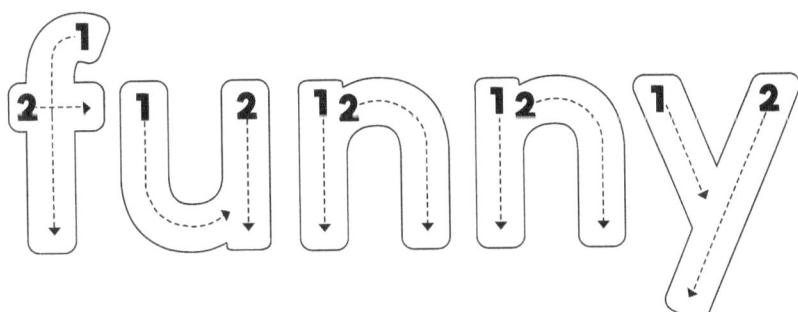

Trace the word:

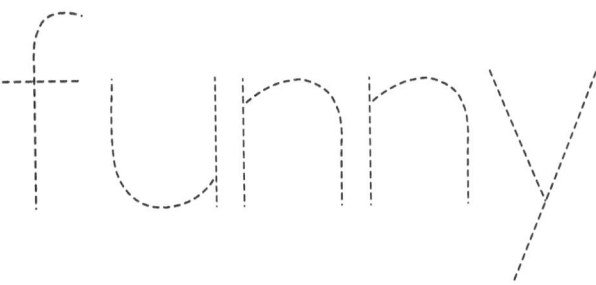

Write the word:

Read the word:

Color the word:

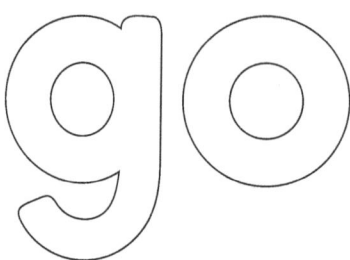

Trace the word:

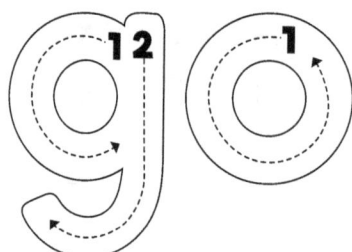

Trace the word:

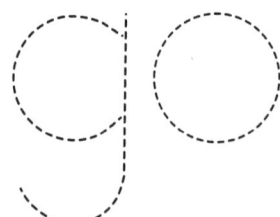

Write the word:

Read the word:

help

Color the word:

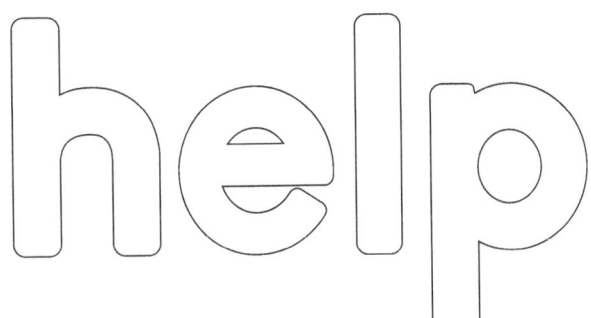

Trace the word:

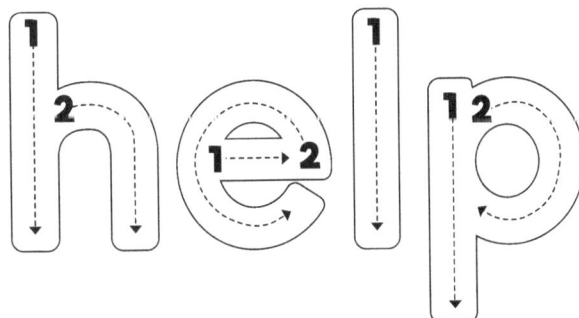

Trace the word:

Write the word:

Read the word:

here

Color the word:

Trace the word:

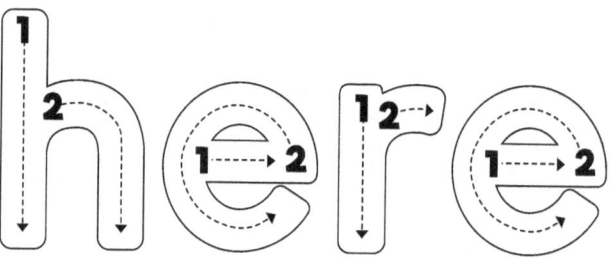

Trace the word:

Write the word:

Read the word:

Color the word:

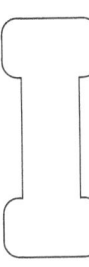

Trace the word:

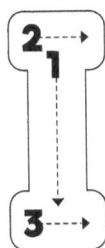

Trace the word:

Write the word:

Read the word:

Color the word:

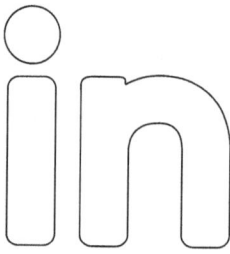

Trace the word:

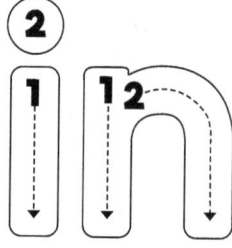

Trace the word:

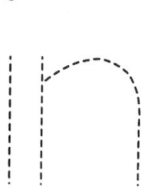

Write the word:

Read the word:

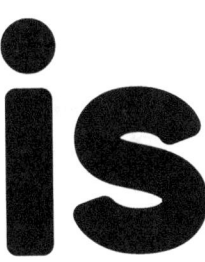

Color the word:

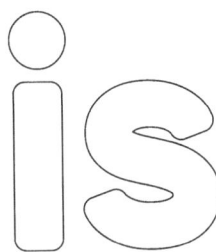

Trace the word:

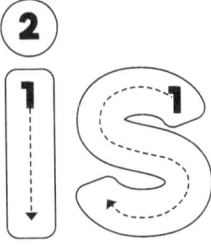

Trace the word:

Write the word:

Read the word:

it

Color the word:

Trace the word:

Trace the word:

Write the word:

Read the word:

Color the word:

Trace the word:

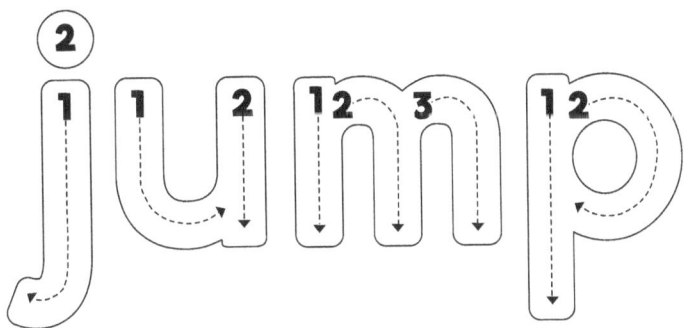

Trace the word:

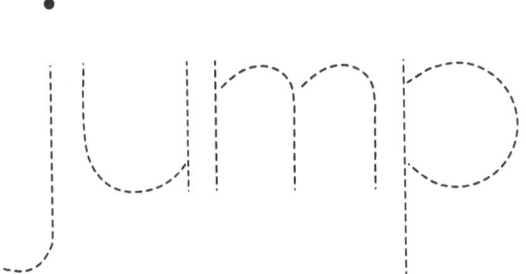

Write the word:

_____

- -

_____

_____

- -

_____

Read the word:

little

Color the word:

Trace the word:

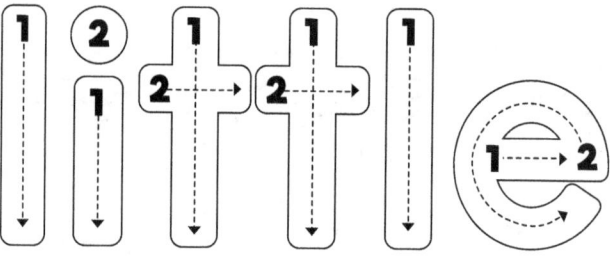

Trace the word:

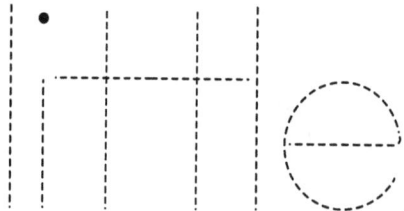

Write the word:

Read the word:

Color the word:

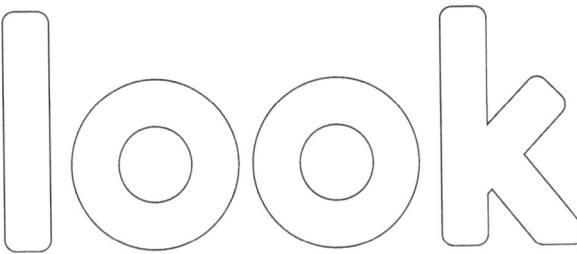

Trace the word:

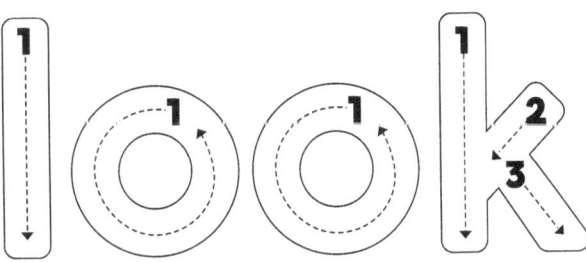

Trace the word:

Write the word:

Read the word:

make

Color the word:

Trace the word:

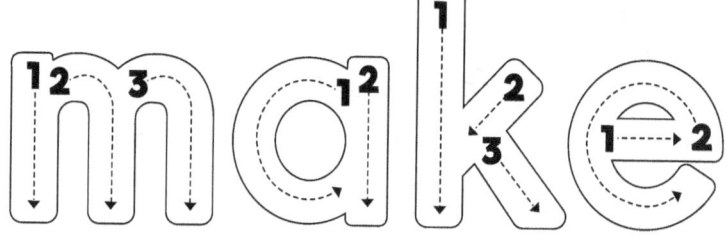

Trace the word:

Write the word:

Read the word:

Color the word:

Trace the word:

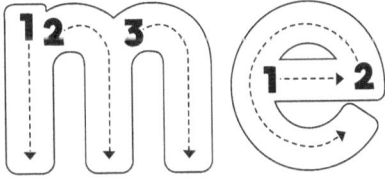

Trace the word:

Write the word:

Read the word:

Color the word:

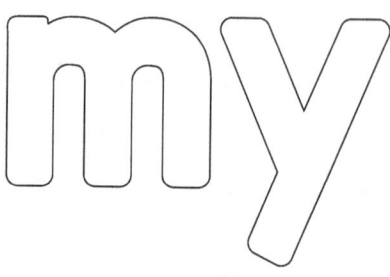

Trace the word:

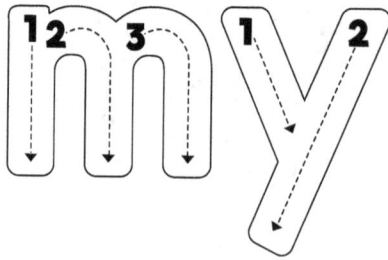

Trace the word:

Write the word:

Read the word:

Color the word:

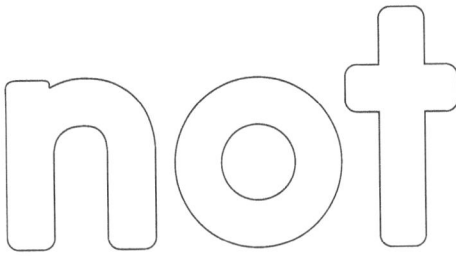

Trace the word:

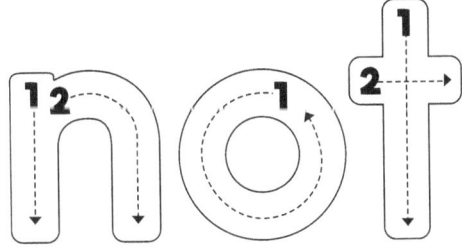

Trace the word:

Write the word:

Read the word:

Color the word:

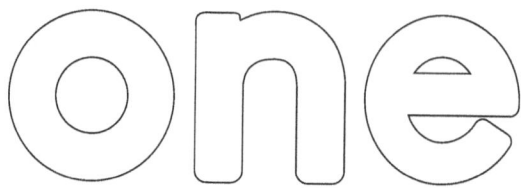

Trace the word:

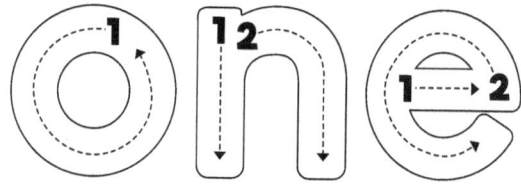

Trace the word:

Write the word:

_____

....

_____

_____

....

_____

Read the word:

Color the word:

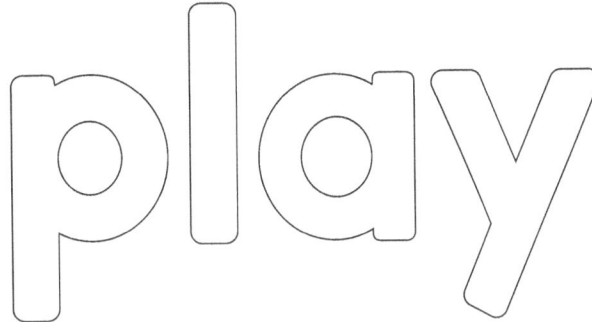

Trace the word:

Trace the word:

Write the word:

Read the word:

red

Color the word:

Trace the word:

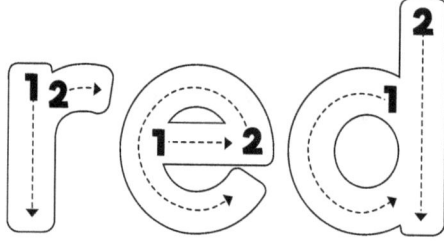

Trace the word:

Write the word:

Read the word:

Color the word:

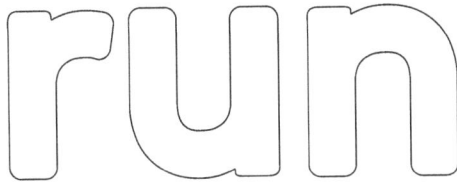

Trace the word:

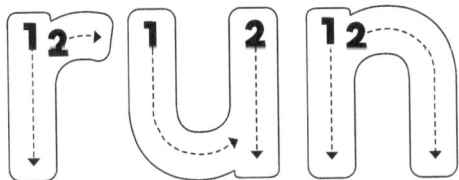

Trace the word:

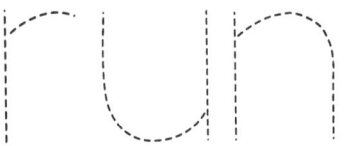

Write the word:

Read the word:

Color the word:

Trace the word:

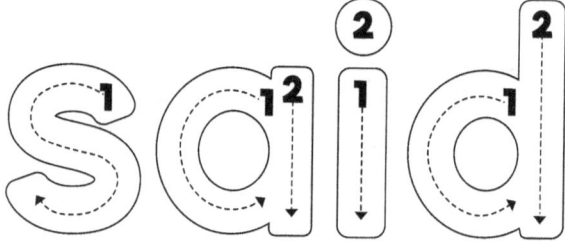

Trace the word:

Write the word:

Read the word:

Color the word:

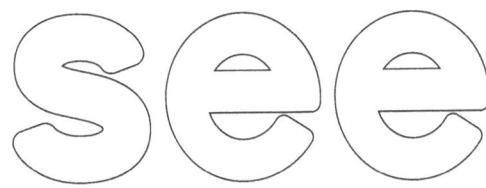

Trace the word:

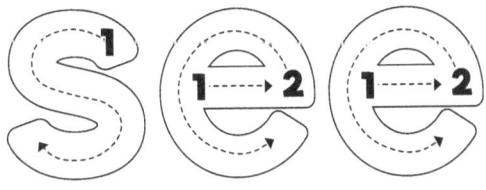

Trace the word:

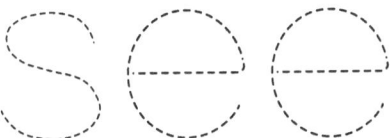

Write the word:

Read the word:

the

Color the word:

Trace the word:

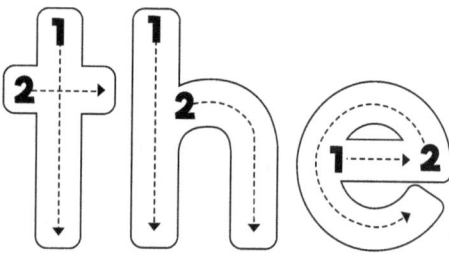

Trace the word:

Write the word:

Read the word:

three

Color the word:

Trace the word:

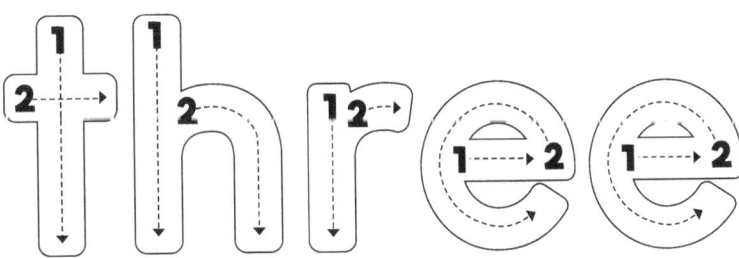

Trace the word:

Write the word:

Read the word:

to

Color the word:

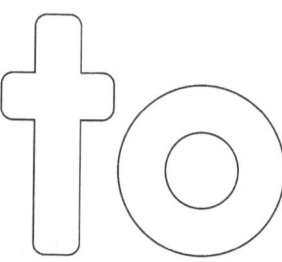

Trace the word:

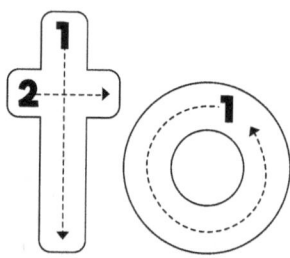

Trace the word:

Write the word:

Read the word:

Color the word:

Trace the word:

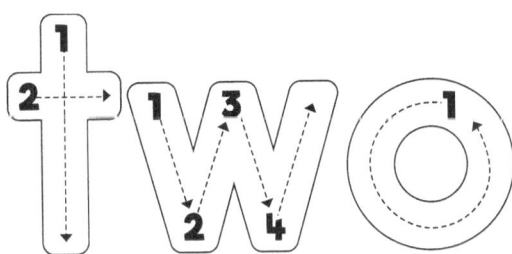

Trace the word:

Write the word:

Read the word:

up

Color the word:

Trace the word:

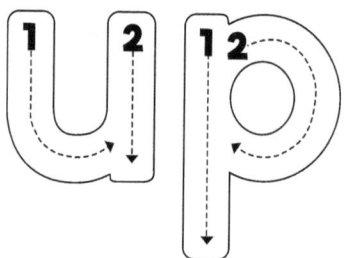

Trace the word:

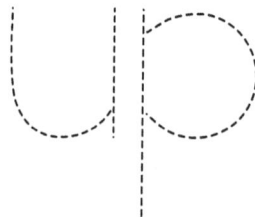

Write the word:

Read the word:

Color the word:

Trace the word:

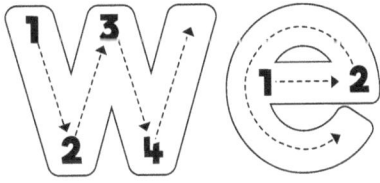

Trace the word:

Write the word:

Read the word:

where

Color the word:

Trace the word:

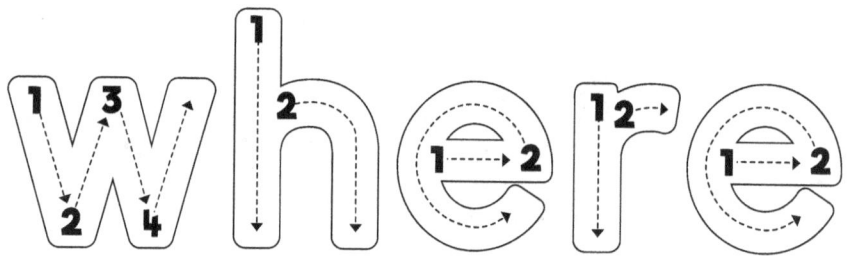

Trace the word:

Write the word:

Read the word:

yellow

Color the word:

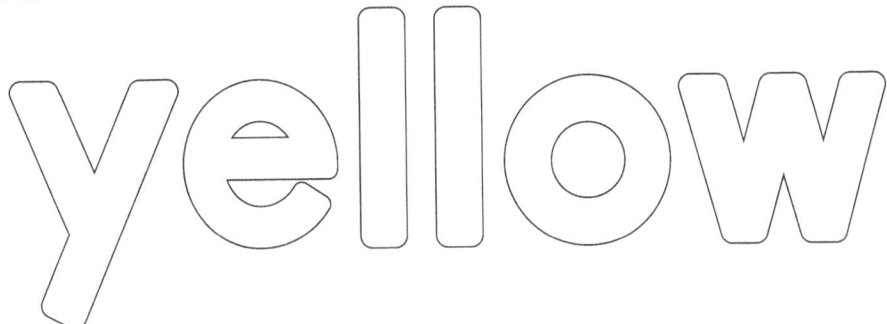

Trace the word:

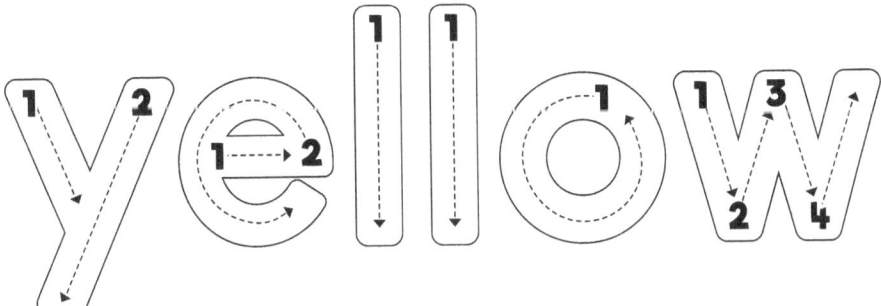

Trace the word:

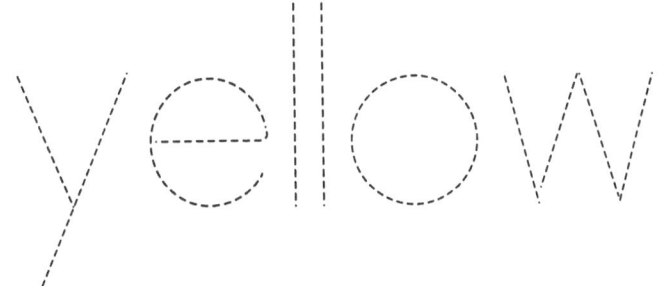

Write the word:

Read the word:

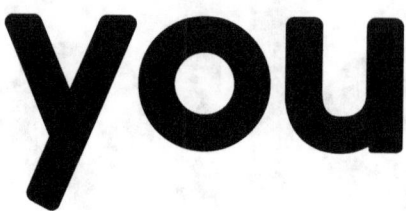

Color the word:

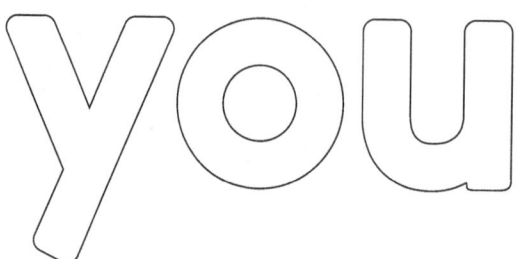

Trace the word:

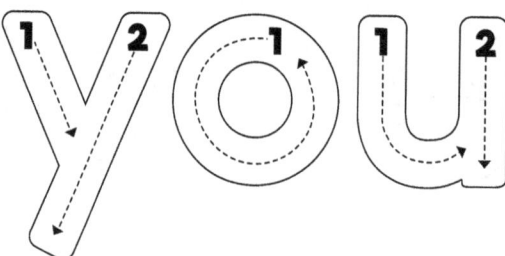

Trace the word:

Write the word:

Kindergarten
Dolch Sight Words

Read the word:

Color the word:

Trace the word:

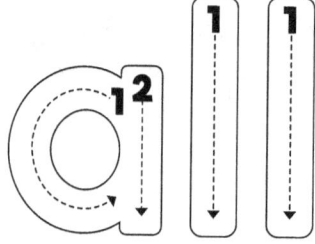

Trace the word:

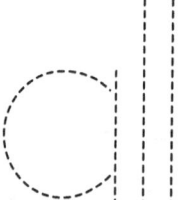

Write the word:

Read the word:

Color the word:

Trace the word:

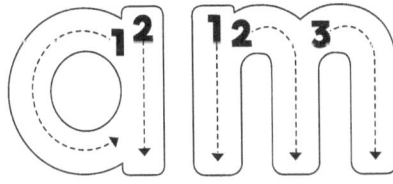

Trace the word:

Write the word:

Read the word:

Color the word:

Trace the word:

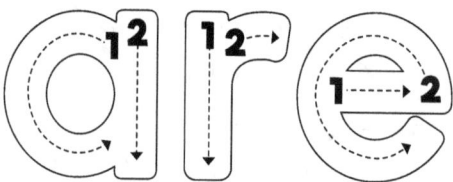

Trace the word:

Write the word:

_____

- -

_____

- -

_____

Read the word:

Color the word:

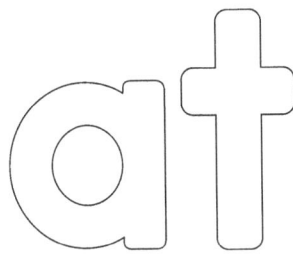

Trace the word:

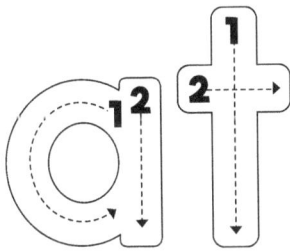

Trace the word:

Write the word:

Read the word:

Color the word:

Trace the word:

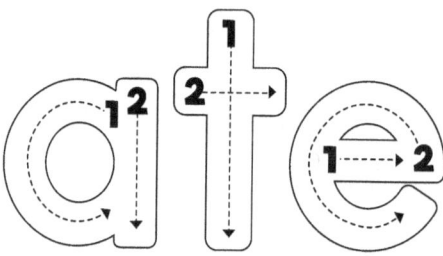

Trace the word:

Write the word:

Read the word:

be

Color the word:

Trace the word:

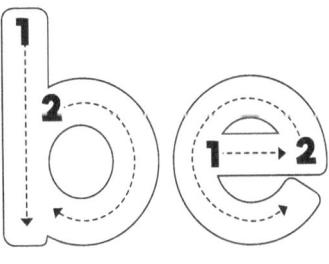

Trace the word:

Write the word:

Read the word:

black

Color the word:

Trace the word:

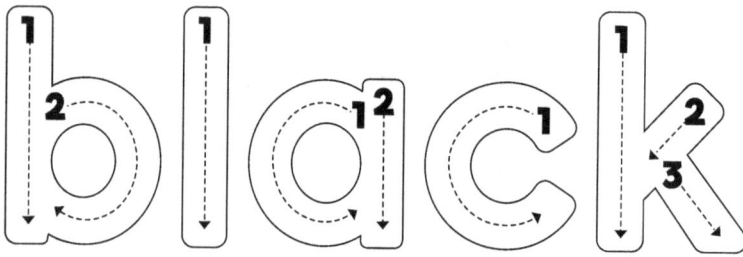

Trace the word:

Write the word:

Read the word:

brown

Color the word:

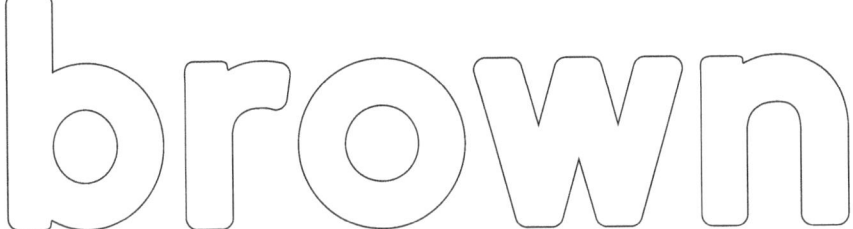

Trace the word:

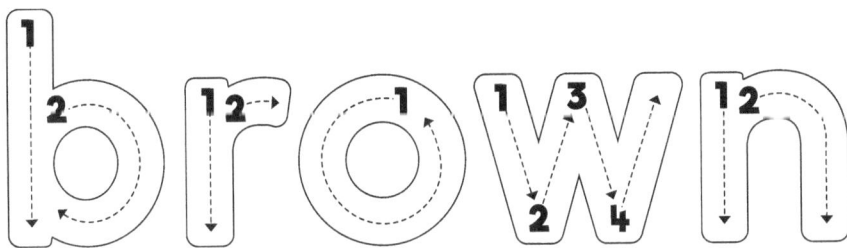

Trace the word:

Write the word: _____

Read the word:

Color the word:

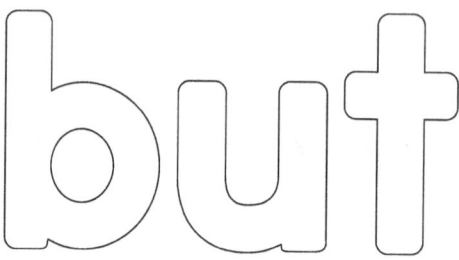

Trace the word:

Trace the word:

Write the word:

_____

_____

_____

_____

Read the word:

Color the word:

Trace the word:

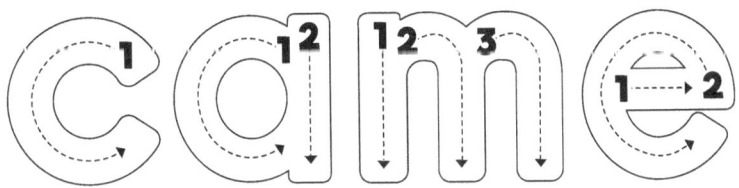

Trace the word:

Write the word: _____

_____

- -

_____

_____

- -

_____

Read the word:

Color the word:

Trace the word:

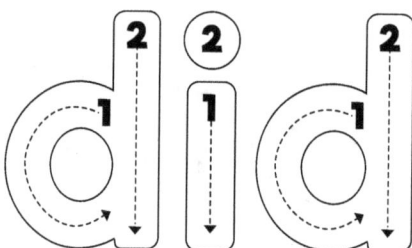

Trace the word:

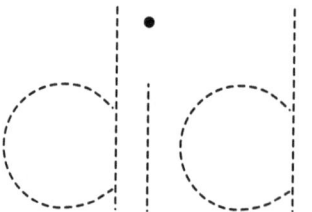

Write the word:

_____

- -

_____

_____

Read the word:

Color the word:

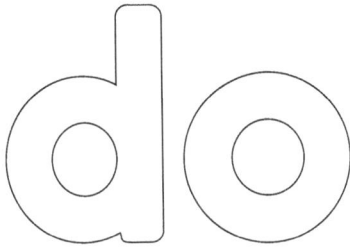

Trace the word:

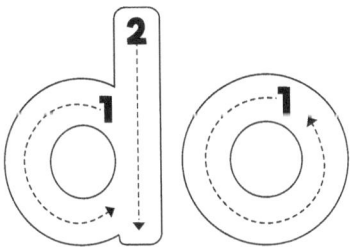

Trace the word:

Write the word: _____

Read the word:

Color the word:

Trace the word:

Trace the word:

Write the word:

Read the word:

Color the word:

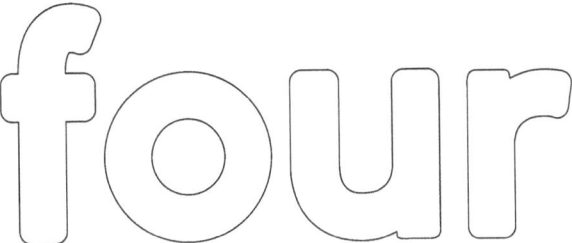

Trace the word:

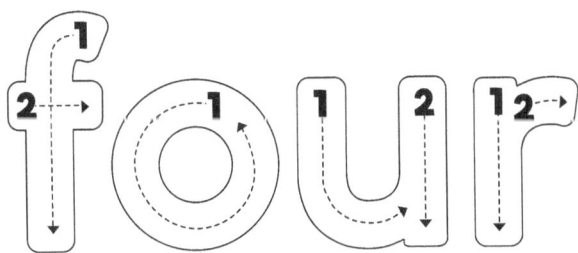

Trace the word:

Write the word:

Read the word:

Color the word:

Trace the word:

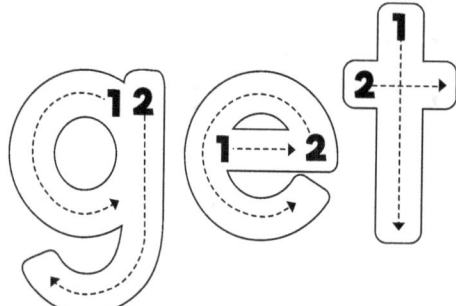

Trace the word:

Write the word:

Read the word:

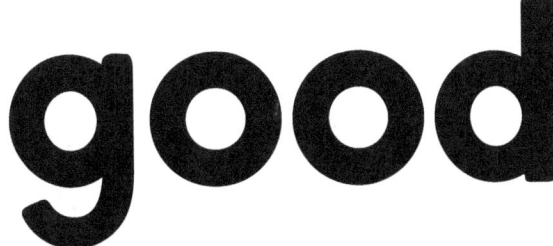

Color the word:

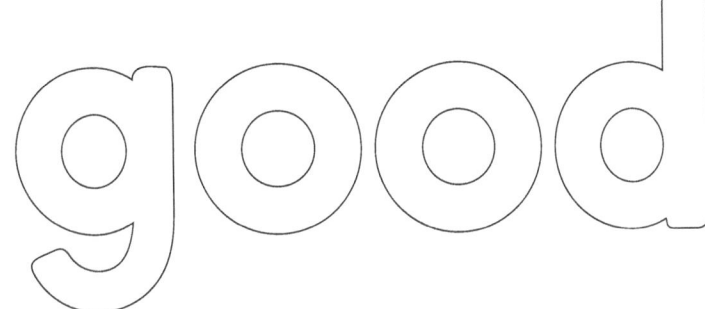

Trace the word:

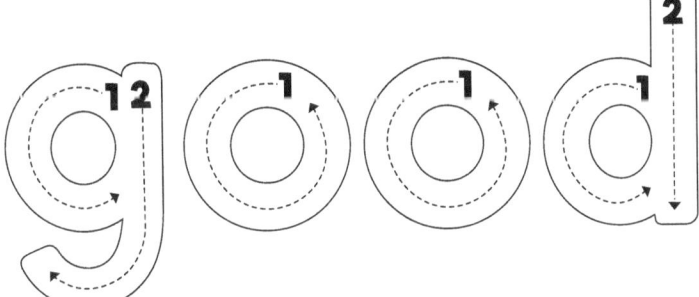

Trace the word:

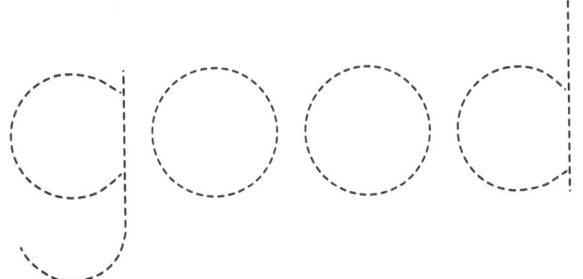

Write the word:

Read the word:

Color the word:

Trace the word:

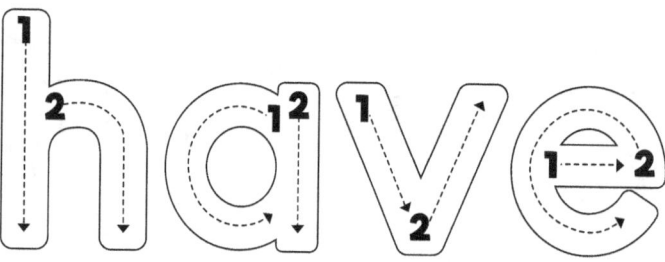

Trace the word:

Write the word:

Read the word:

he

Color the word:

Trace the word:

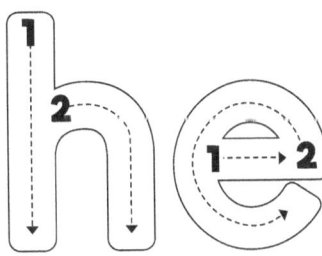

Trace the word:

Write the word:

Read the word:

Color the word:

Trace the word:

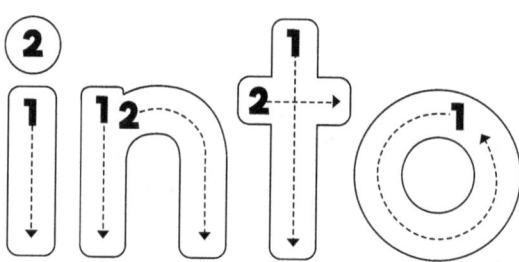

Trace the word:

Write the word:

Read the word:

Color the word:

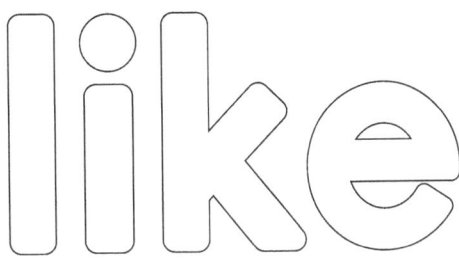

Trace the word:

Trace the word:

Write the word:

Read the word:

Color the word:

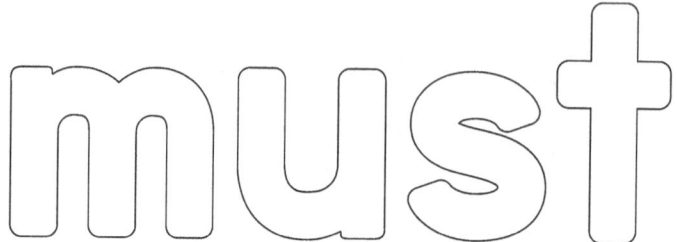

Trace the word:

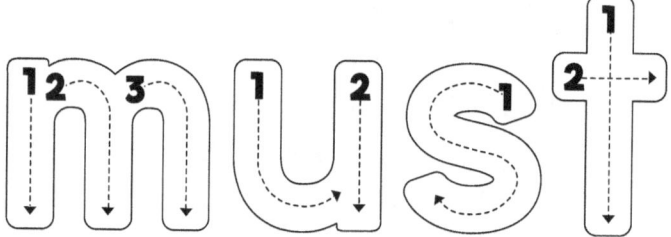

Trace the word:

Write the word:

Read the word:

new

Color the word:

Trace the word:

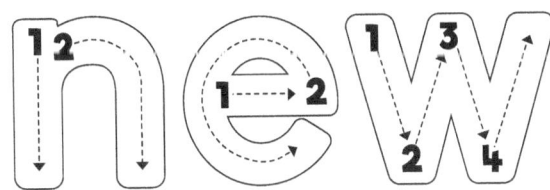

Trace the word:

Write the word: _____

Read the word:

Color the word:

Trace the word:

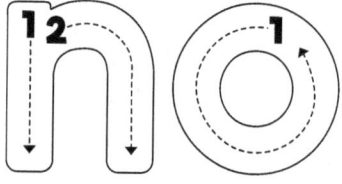

Trace the word:

Write the word:

Read the word:

Color the word:

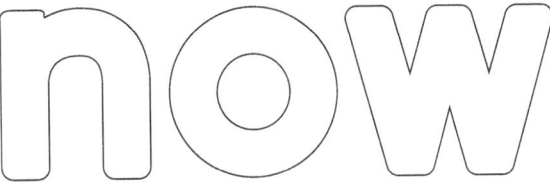

Trace the word:

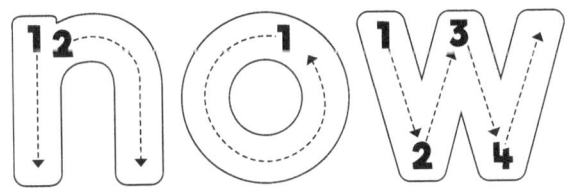

Trace the word:

Write the word:

Read the word:

Color the word:

Trace the word:

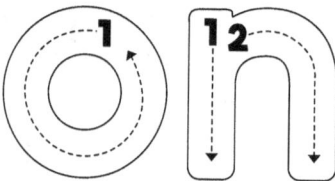

Trace the word:

Write the word:

Read the word:

Color the word:

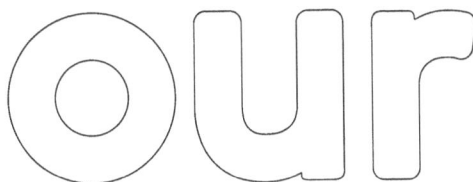

Trace the word:

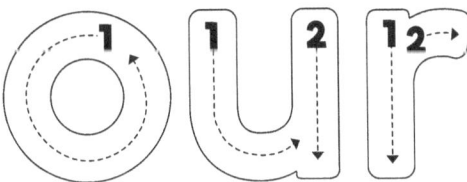

Trace the word:

Write the word:

Read the word:

Color the word:

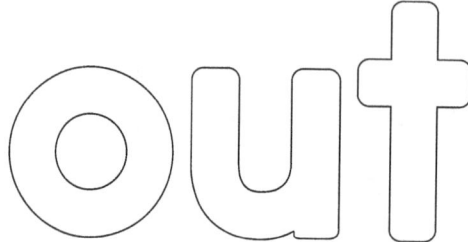

Trace the word:

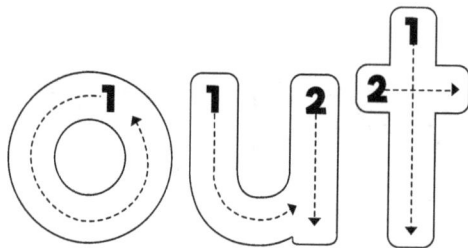

Trace the word:

Write the word:

Read the word:

please

Color the word:

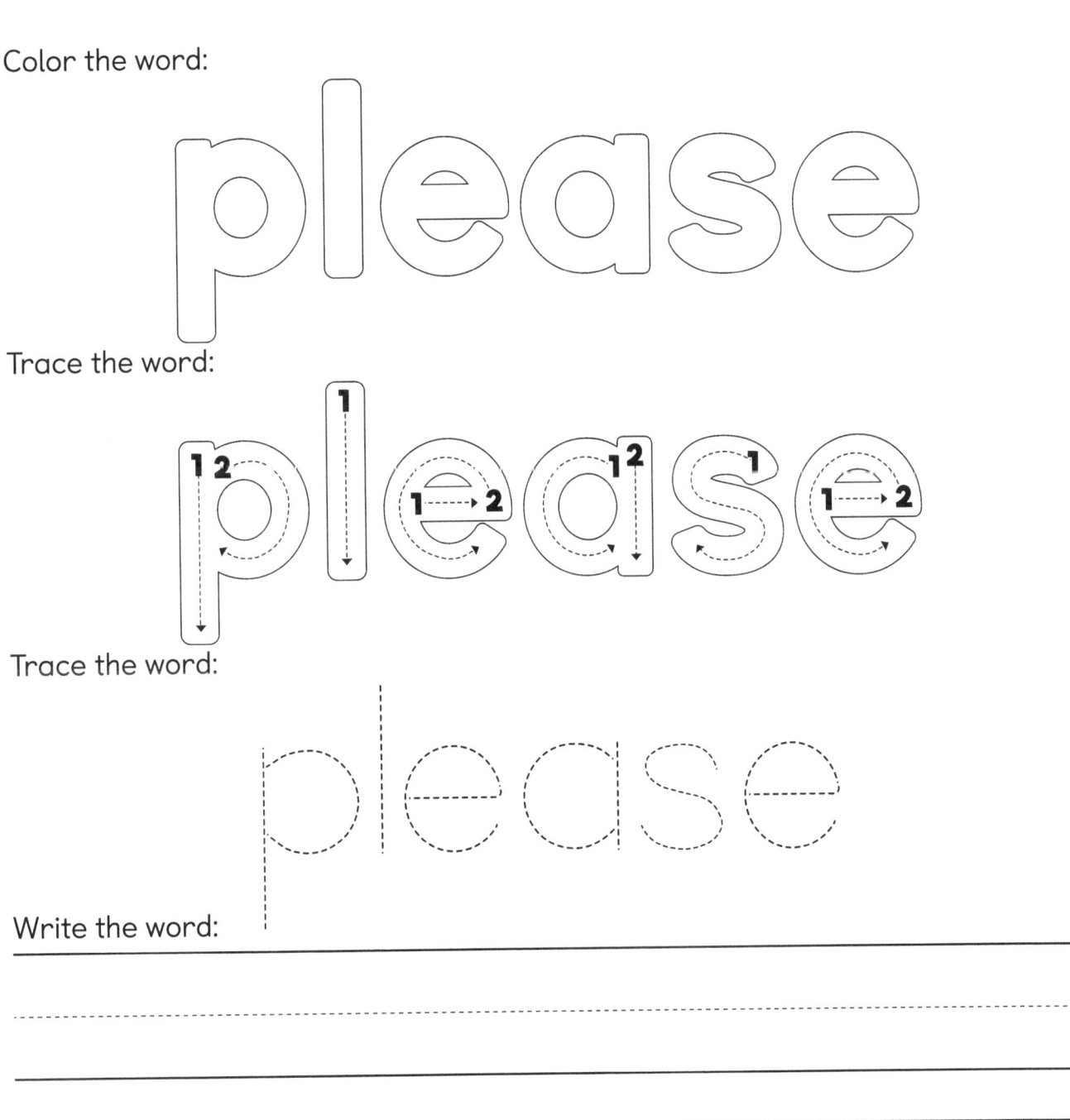

Trace the word:

Trace the word:

Write the word:

Read the word:

Color the word:

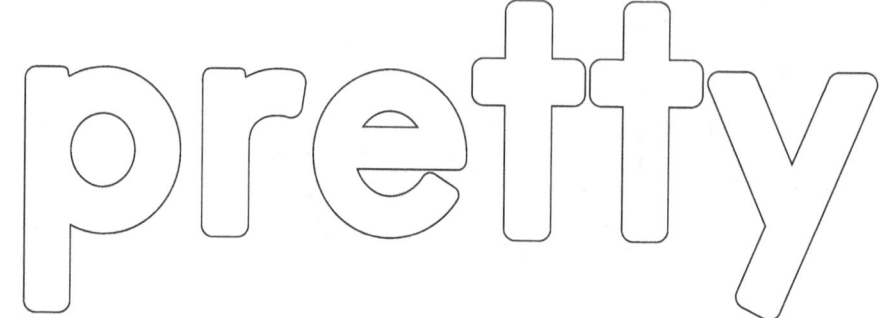

Trace the word:

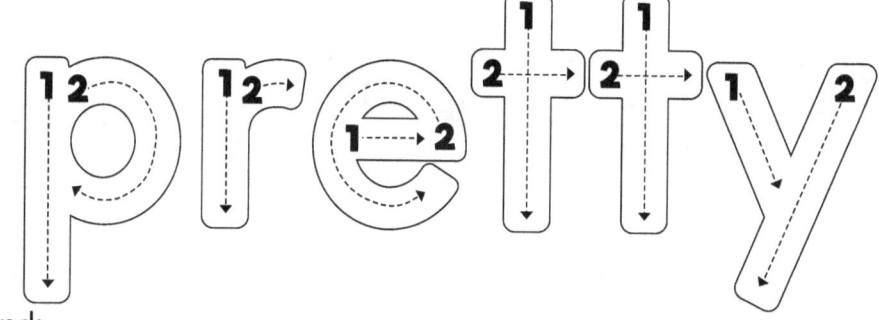

Trace the word:

Write the word:

Read the word:

Color the word:

Trace the word:

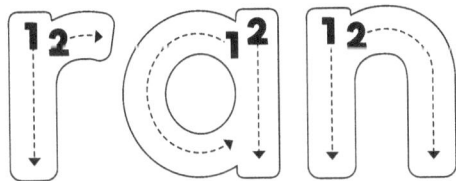

Trace the word:

Write the word:

Read the word:

Color the word:

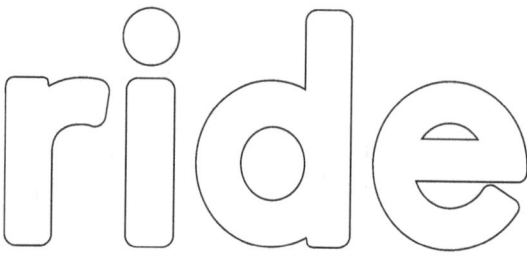

Trace the word:

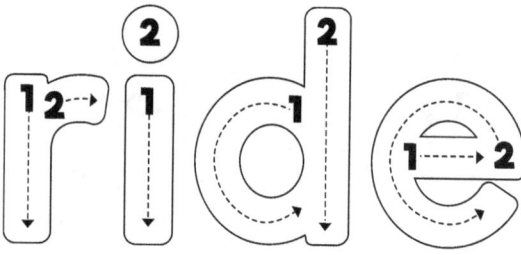

Trace the word:

Write the word:

Read the word:

Color the word:

Trace the word:

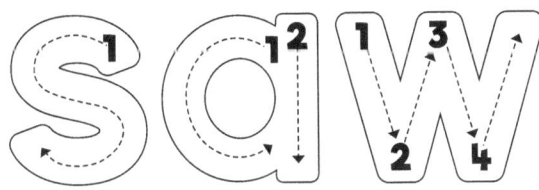

Trace the word:

Write the word:

Read the word:

Color the word:

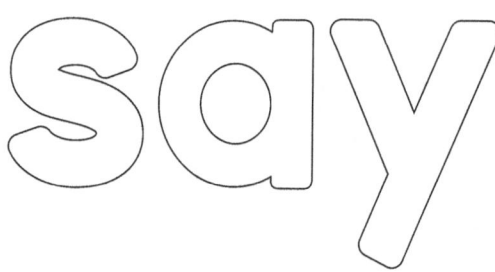

Trace the word:

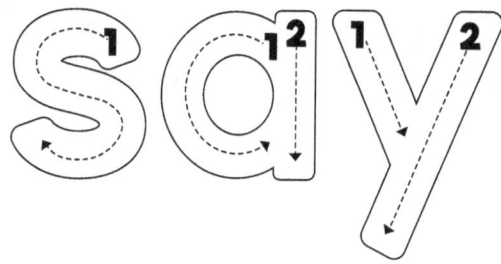

Trace the word:

Write the word:

Read the word:

she

Color the word:

Trace the word:

Trace the word:

Write the word: _____

- -

_____

- -

_____

Read the word:

Color the word:

Trace the word:

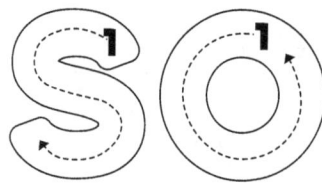

Trace the word:

Write the word:

Read the word:

Color the word:

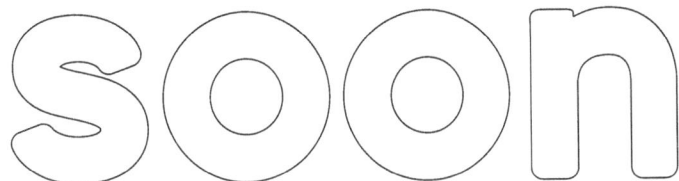

Trace the word:

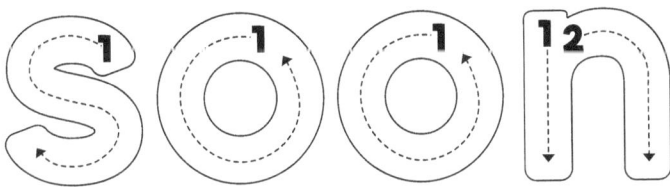

Trace the word:

Write the word:

Read the word:

Color the word:

Trace the word:

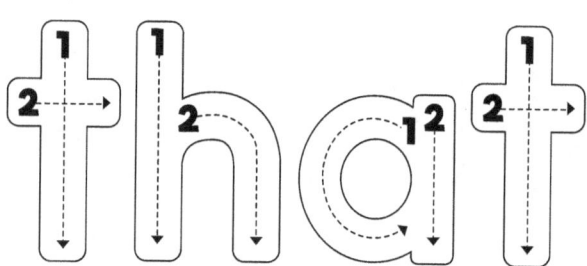

Trace the word:

Write the word:

Read the word:

there

Color the word:

Trace the word:

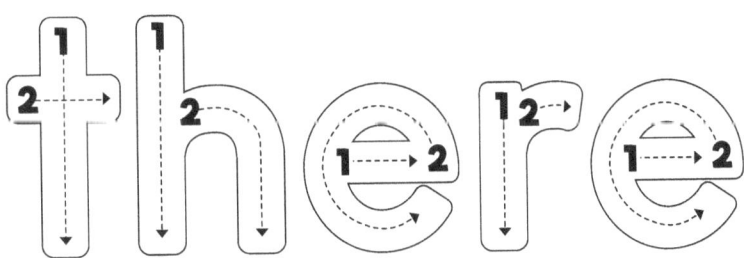

Trace the word:

Write the word: _____

_____

_____

_____

Read the word:

Color the word:

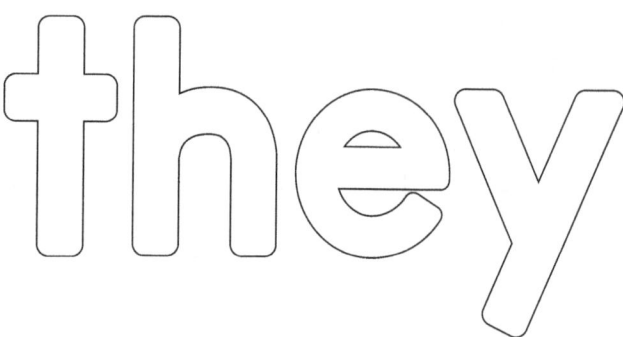

Trace the word:

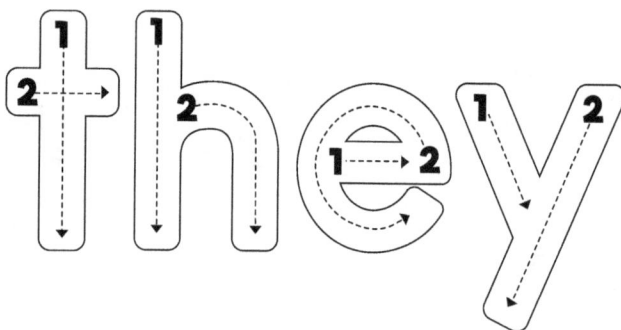

Trace the word:

Write the word:

Read the word:

this

Color the word:

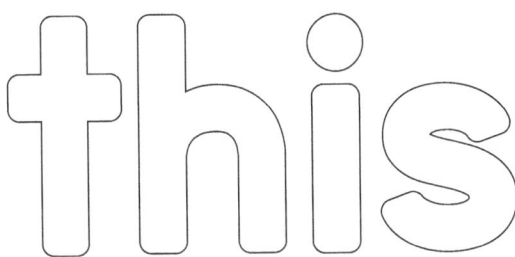

Trace the word:

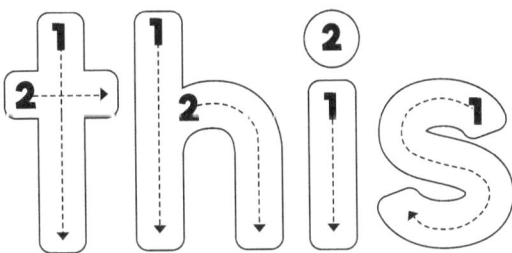

Trace the word:

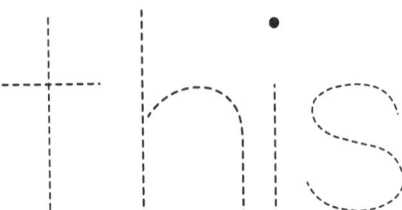

Write the word:

Read the word:

Color the word:

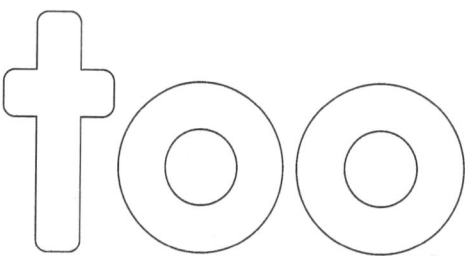

Trace the word:

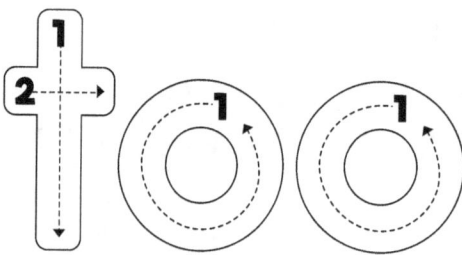

Trace the word:

Write the word:

Read the word:

under

Color the word:

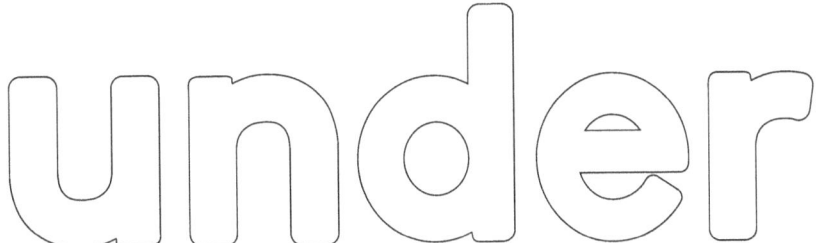

Trace the word:

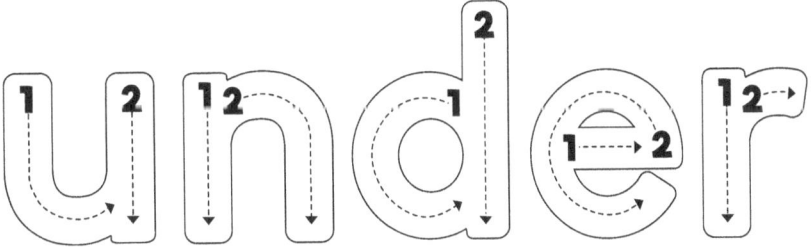

Trace the word:

Write the word:

Read the word:

Color the word:

Trace the word:

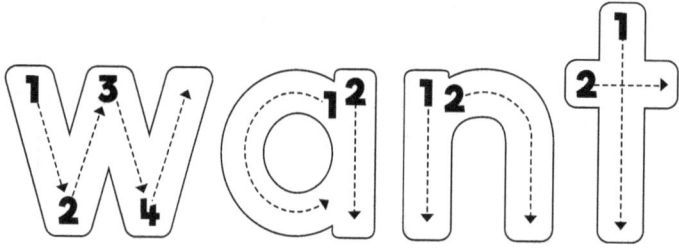

Trace the word:

Write the word:

Read the word:

Color the word:

Trace the word:

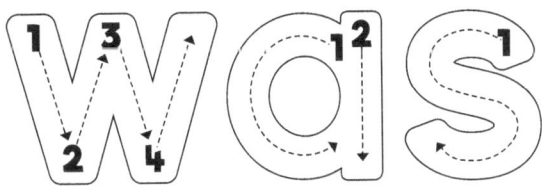

Trace the word:

Write the word:

Read the word:

Color the word:

Trace the word:

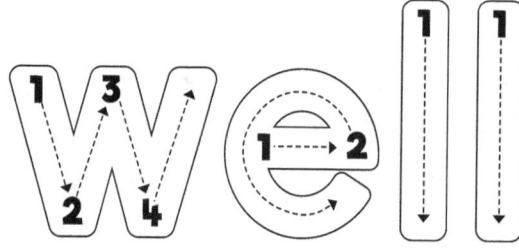

Trace the word:

Write the word:

_____

- -

_____

_____

- -

_____

Read the word:

went

Color the word:

Trace the word:

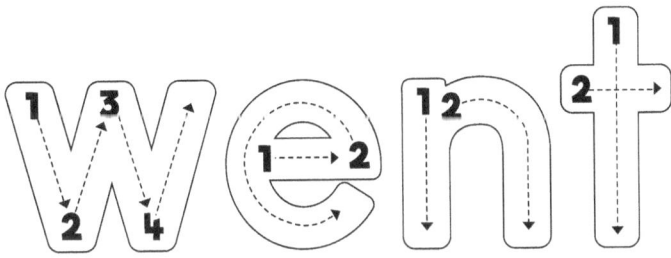

Trace the word:

Write the word: _____

....

_____

_____

....

_____

Read the word:

Color the word:

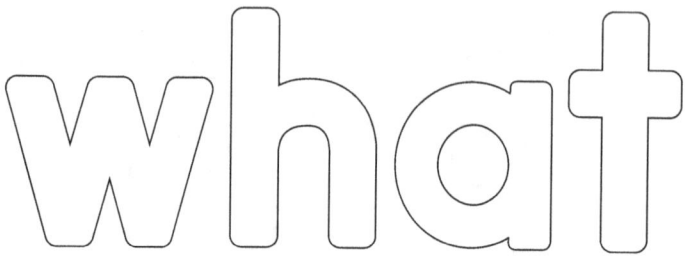

Trace the word:

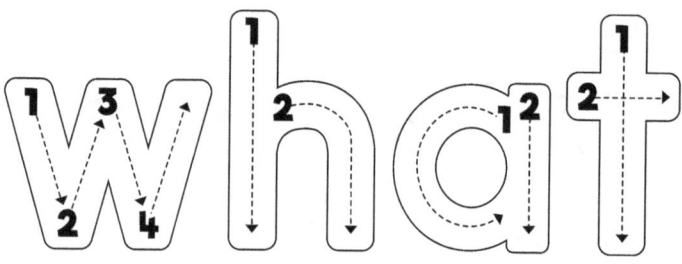

Trace the word:

Write the word:

Read the word:

Color the word:

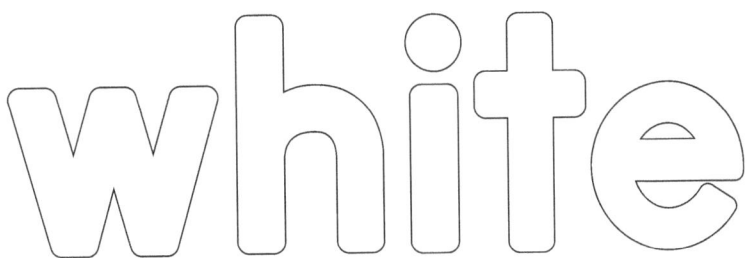

Trace the word:

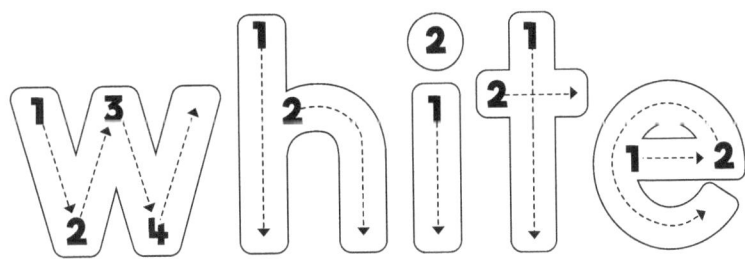

Trace the word:

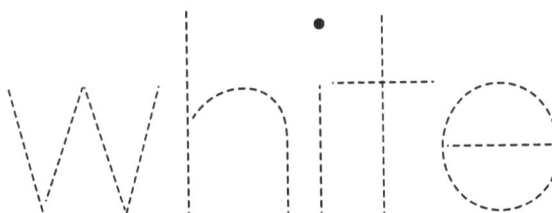

Write the word:

Read the word:

Color the word:

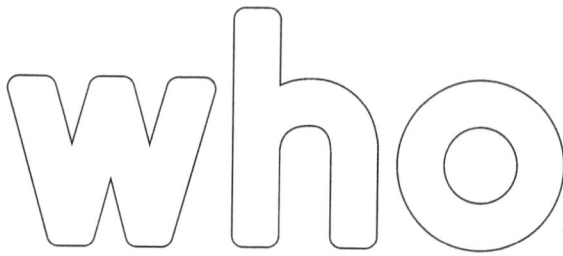

Trace the word:

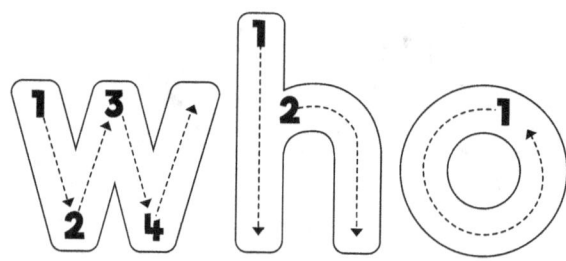

Trace the word:

Write the word:

Read the word:

Color the word:

Trace the word:

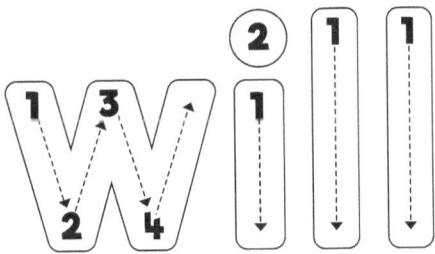

Trace the word:

Write the word:

Read the word:

Color the word:

Trace the word:

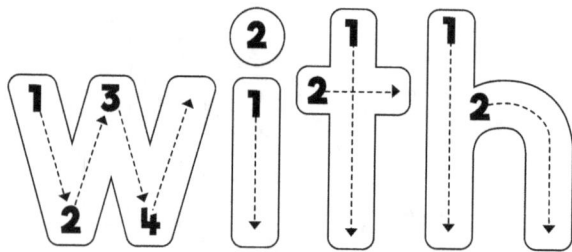

Trace the word:

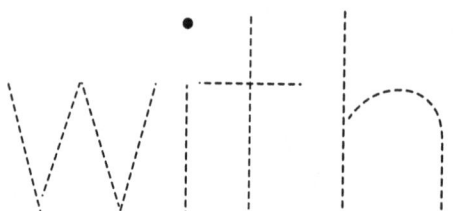

Write the word:

Read the word:

Color the word:

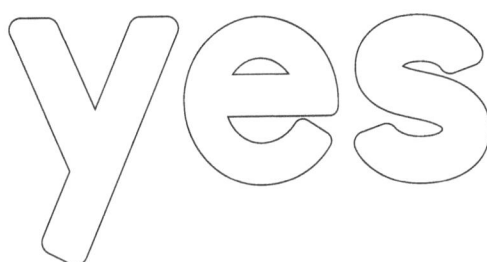

Trace the word:

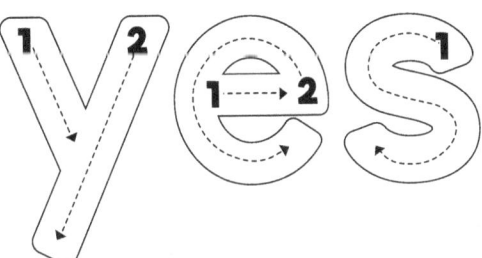

Trace the word:

Write the word:

Pre-K & Kindergarten

Dolch Sight Words

Flashcards

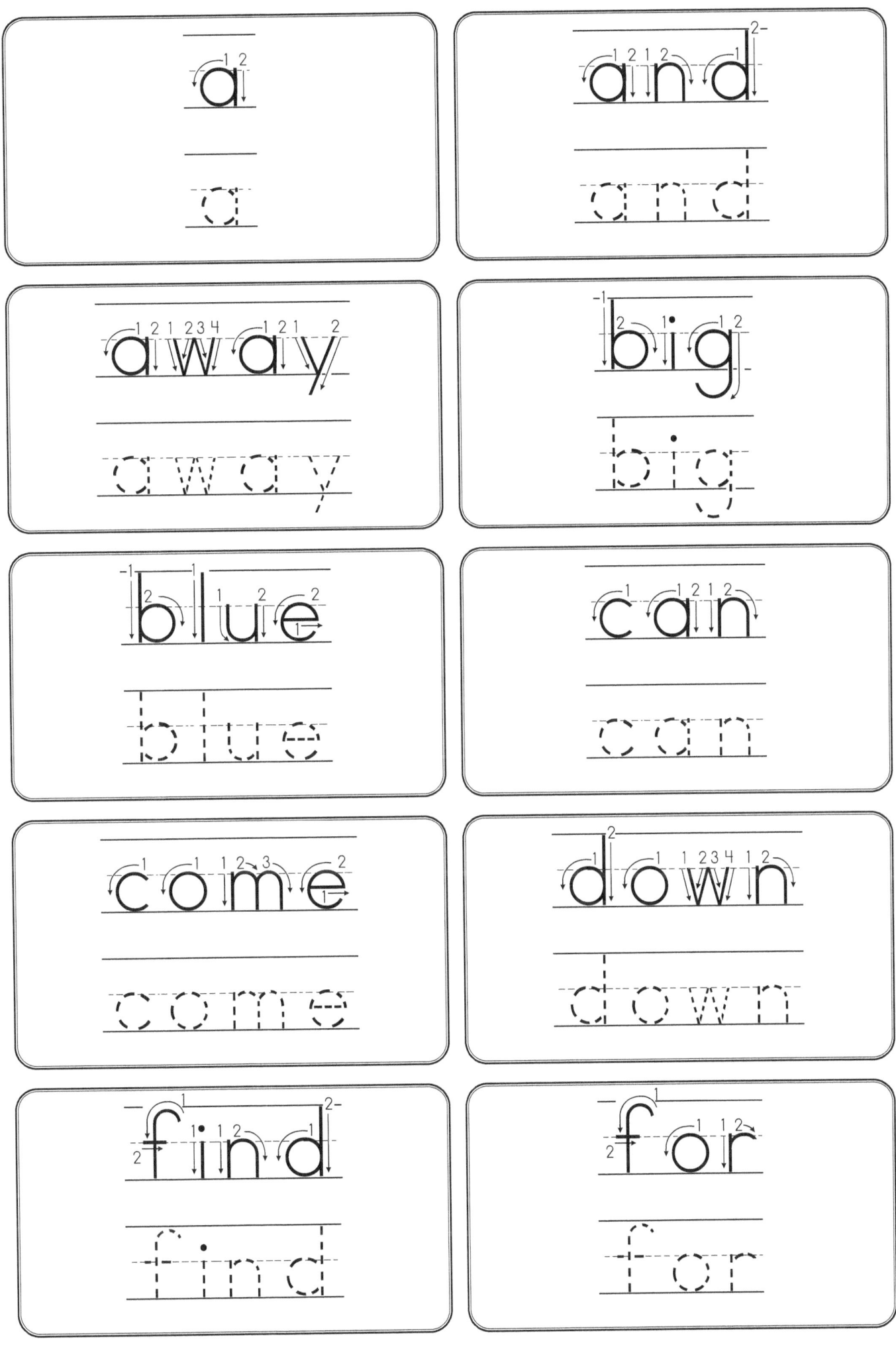

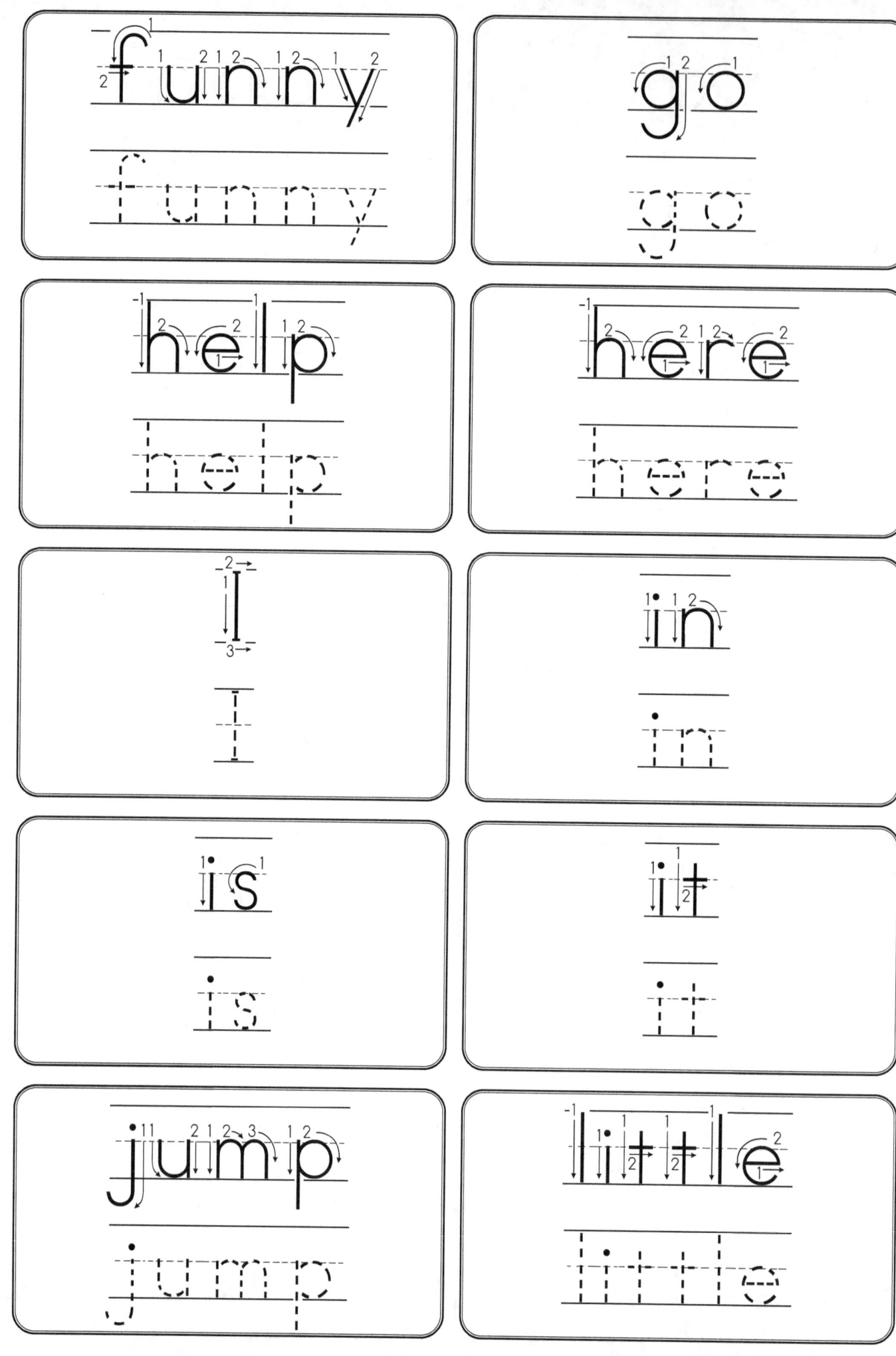

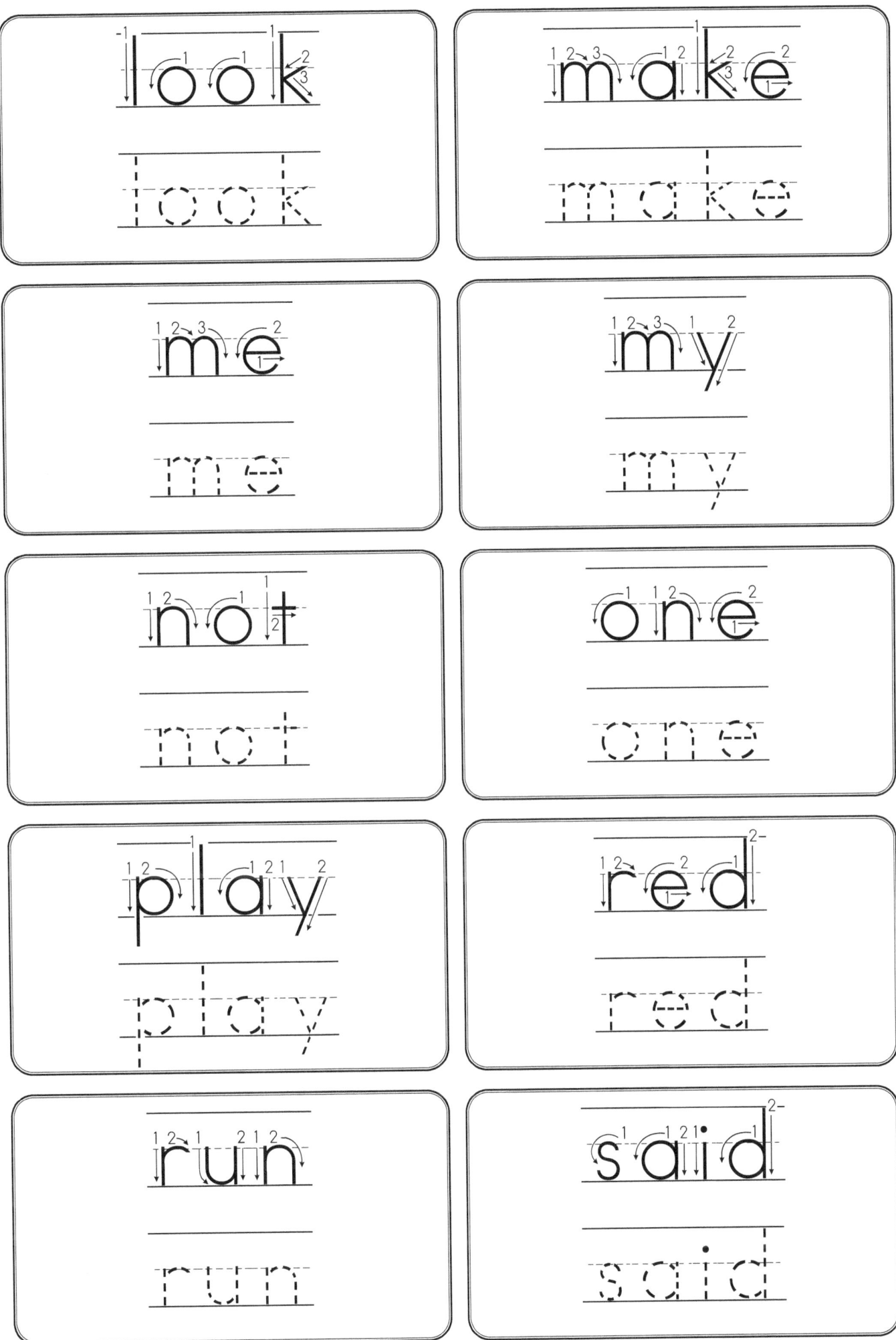

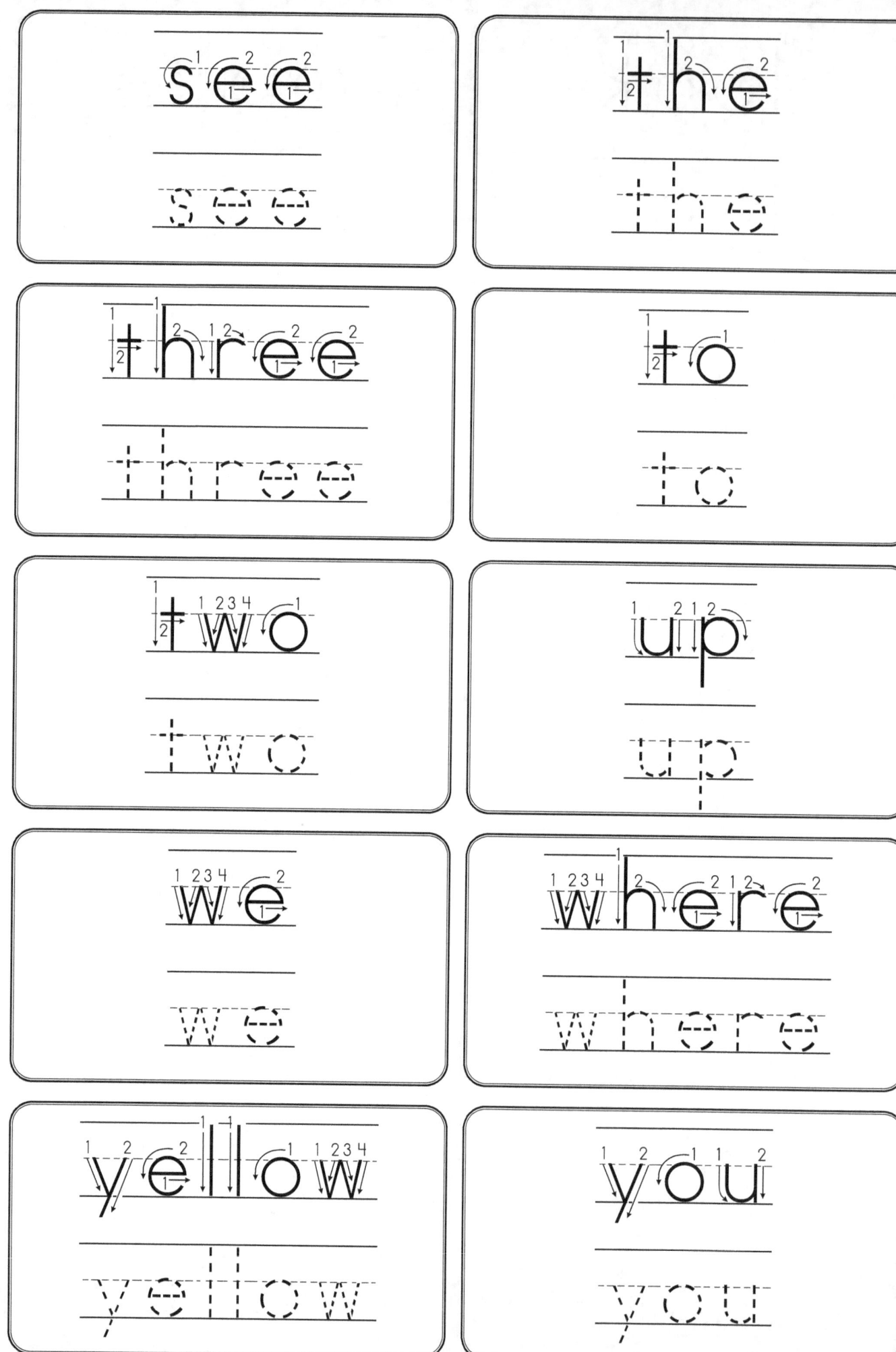

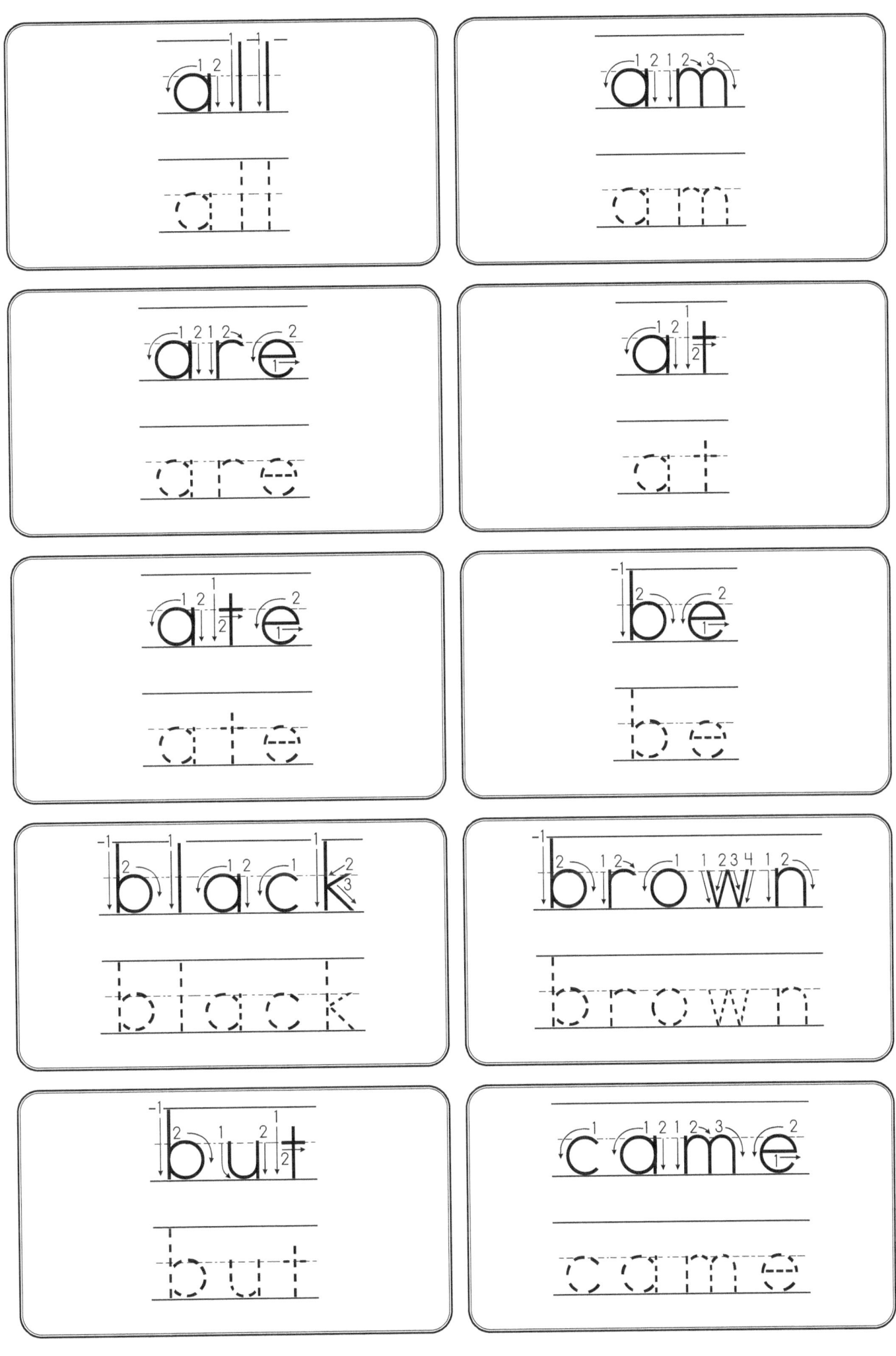

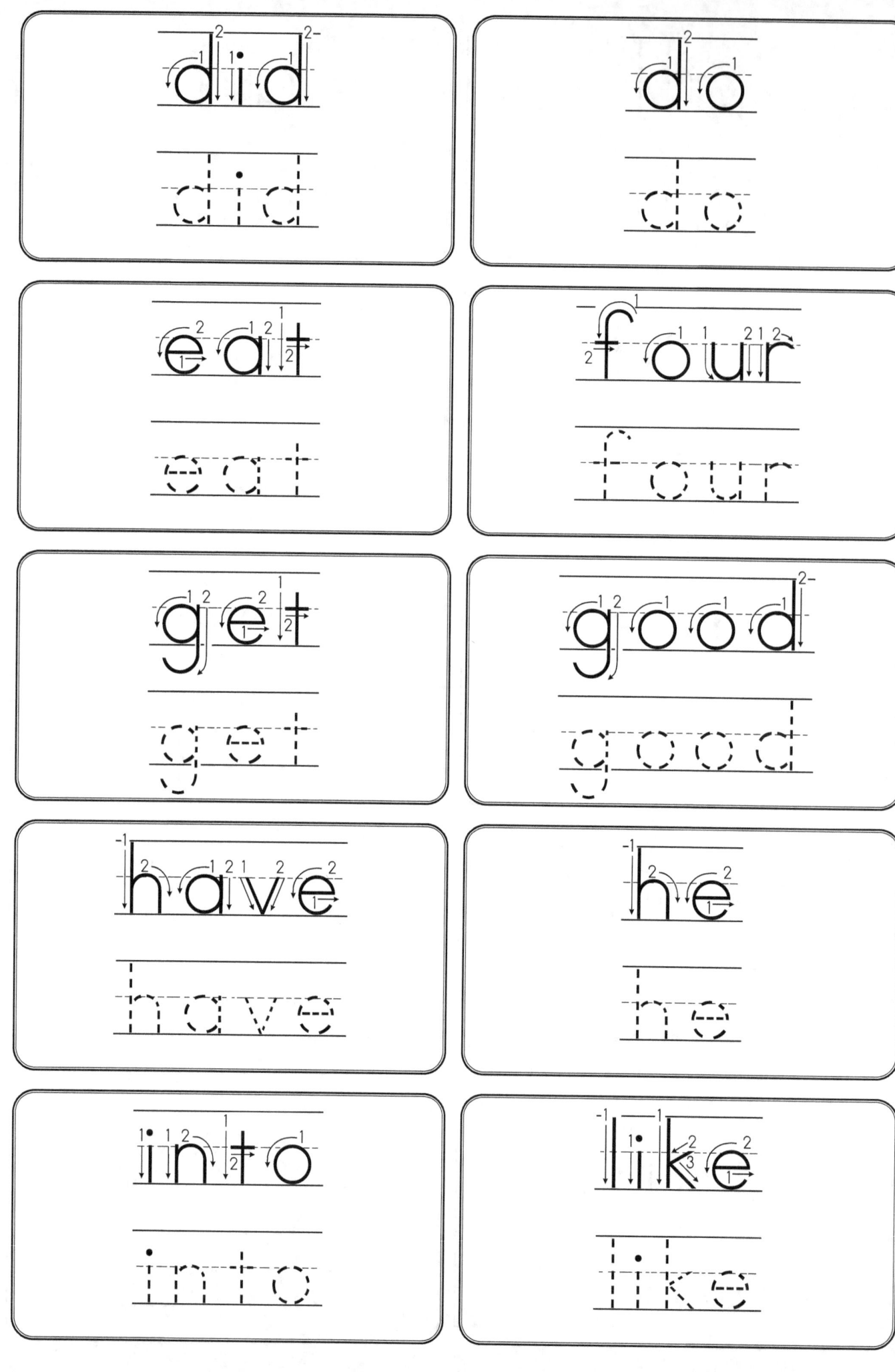

must

must

new

new

no

no

now

now

on

on

our

our

out

out

please

please

pretty

pretty

ran

ran

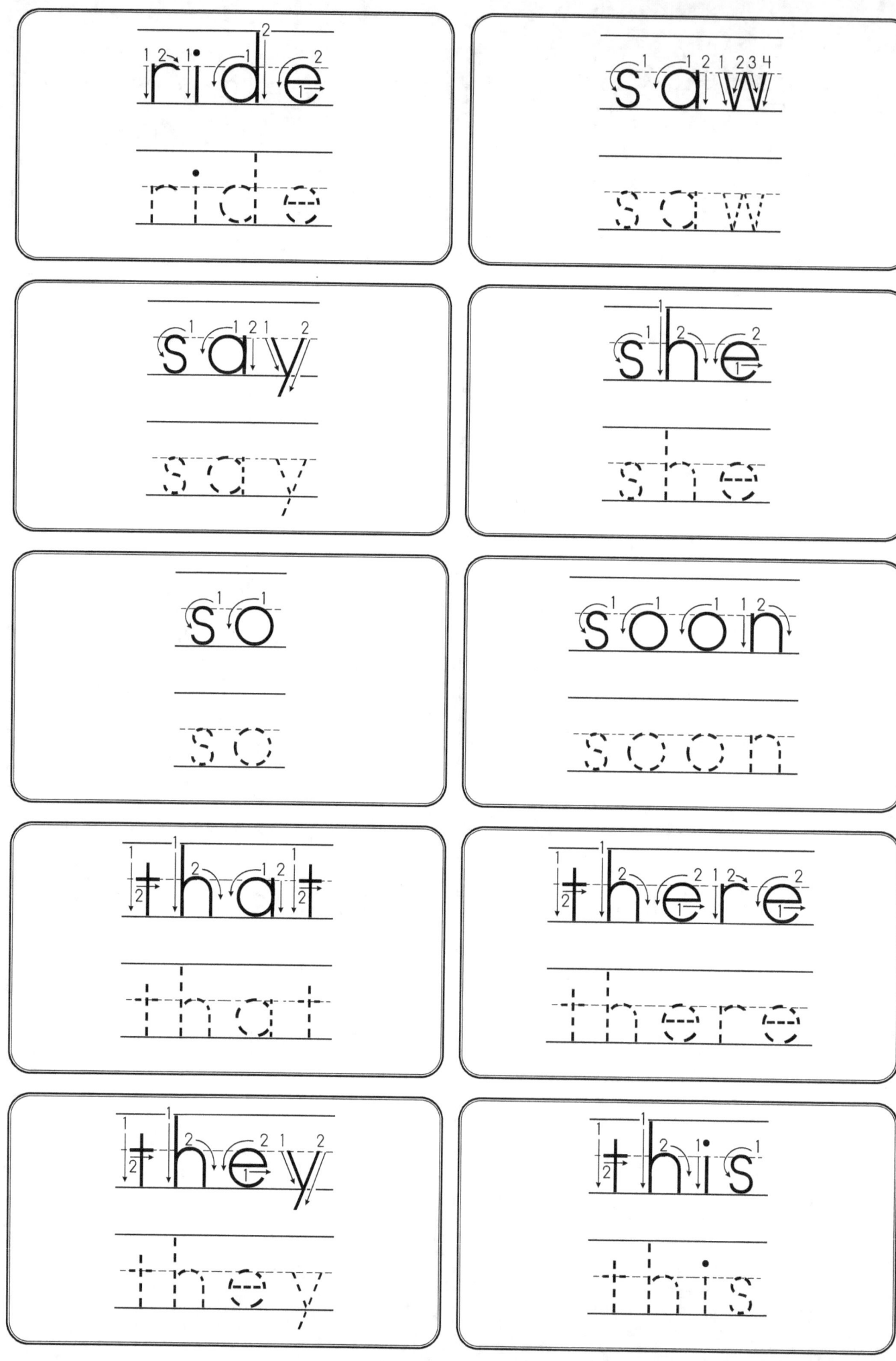

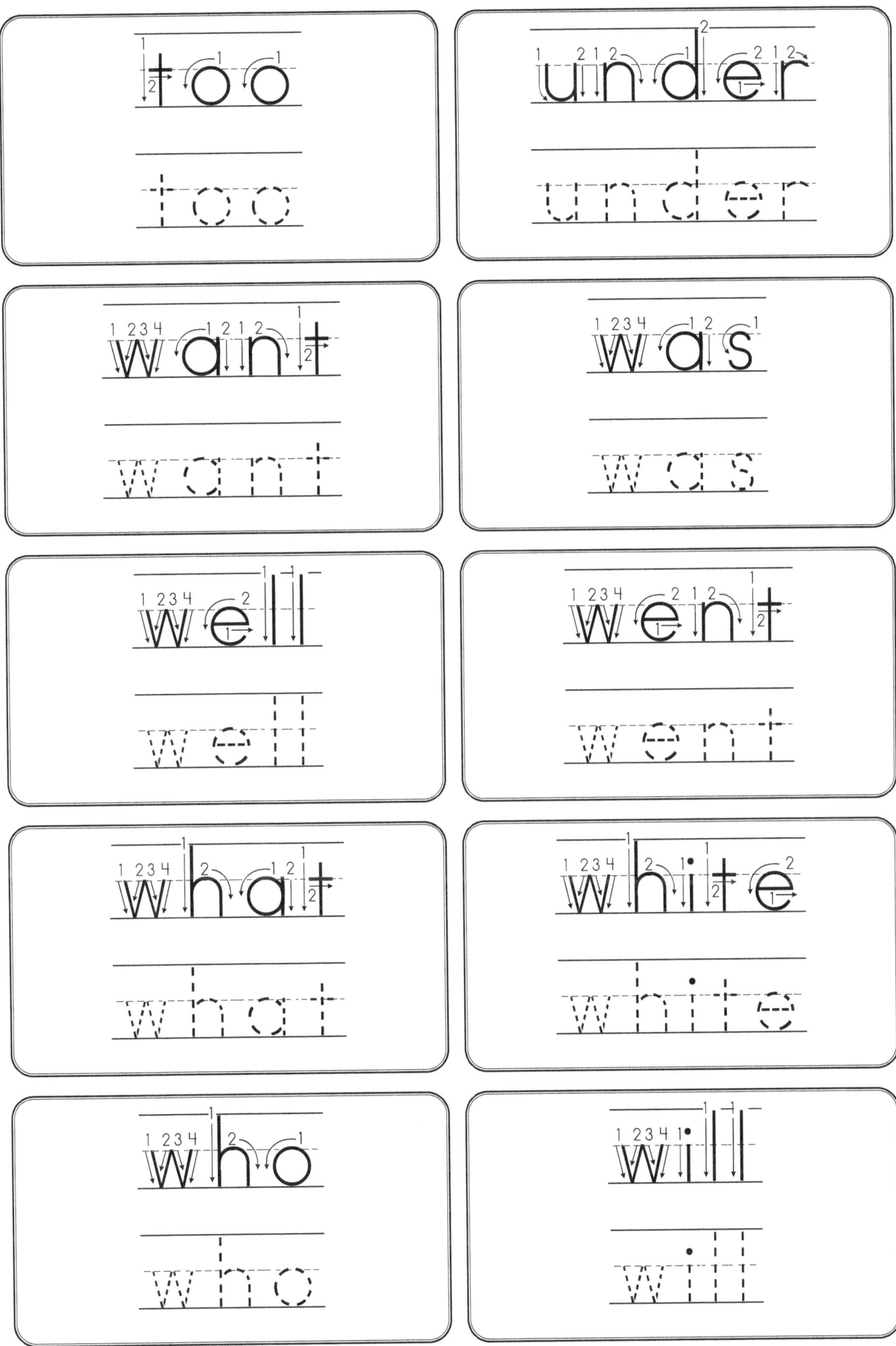

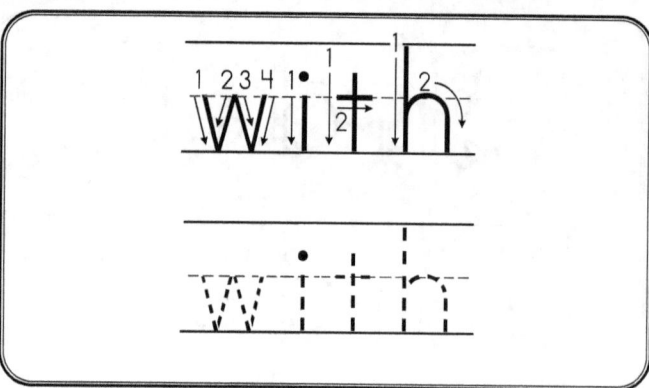

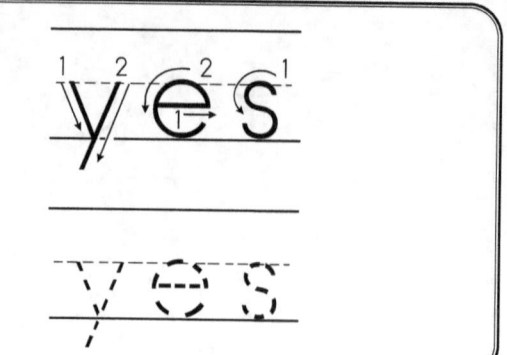

Dolch Pre-Kindergarten Sight Words

a	and	away	big	blue
can	come	down	find	for
funny	go	help	here	I
in	is	it	jump	little
look	make	me	my	not
one	play	red	run	said
see	the	three	to	two
up	we	where	yellow	you

Dolch Kindergarten Sight Words

all	am	are	at	ate
be	black	brown	but	came
did	do	eat	four	get
good	have	he	into	like
must	new	no	now	on
our	out	please	pretty	ran
ride	saw	say	she	so
soon	that	there	they	this
too	under	want	was	well
went	what	white	who	will
with	yes			

Check out our other books!

abcZbook Press

Congratulations!

Dolch

DIPLOMA in
Pre-K & Kindergarten
Sight Words

You are a SuperStar!

abcZbook

By:

Date: